Spaghetti with Grape Tomatoes and Pesto *page 174*

Italian Sausage Soup *page 22*

Spice-Rubbed Ribs with Roasted Corn *page 208*

Penne with Gruyère and Cremini Mushrooms *page 176*

Smoke and Spice Mussel Chowder *page 18*

Farmhouse Chicken Pot Pie *page 64*

Spanish Chicken and Garbanzo Stew *page 142*

Chicken, Basil, and Peanut Stir-Fry *page 100*

Roast Jerk Pork with Yams and Watercress *page 206*

Warm Salmon, Asparagus, and Scallion Salad *page 42*

Risotto with Saffron, Shrimp, and Peas *page 188*

Roast Beef and Vegetable Dinner *page 194*

Sliced Steak, Baby Spinach, and Roquefort Salad *page 48*

Quick Cassoulet *page 58*

Pork Tenderloin and Bell Pepper Stir-Fry *page 120*

The Simpler The Better

Sensational One-Dish Meals

THE SIMPLER THE BETTER

Sensational Home Cooking in 3 Easy Steps

Sensational Italian Meals

Sensational One-Dish Meals

The Simpler The Better

SENSATIONAL ONE-DISH MEALS

LESLIE REVSIN

with Rick Rodgers

JOHN WILEY & SONS, INC.

Published by John Wiley & Sons, Inc., Hoboken, New Jersey

Published simultaneously in Canada

For general information on our other products and services or for technical support, please contact our Customer Care Department within the United States at 800-762-2974, outside the United States at (317) 572-3993 or fax (317) 572-4002.

Wiley also publishes its books in a variety of electronic formats. Some content that appears in print may not be available in electronic books. For more information about Wiley products, visit our web site at www.wiley.com.

LIBRARY OF CONGRESS CATALOGING-IN-PUBLICATION DATA:

Revsin, Leslie.
  The simpler the better : sensational one-dish meals /
Leslie Revsin.
    p. cm.
  Includes index.
  ISBN 0-471-48233-1 (pbk.)
  1. One-dish meals. 2. Quick and easy cookery. I. Title: Sensational
one-dish meals. II. Title.
  TX840.O53R48 2005
  641.5'55‹\m›dc22

2004019933

Book Design by Richard Oriolo
Photography Copyright © 2005 by Duane Winfield
Food Styling by Megan Fawn Schlow
Prop Styling by Duane Winfield and Justin Schwartz

Printed in the United States of America
10 9 8 7 6 5 4 3 2 1

To the Susans,

Ginsburg and Wyler,

for the years of friendship

and support

Contents

From the Pot: Stews, Ragùs, and Chilies

These fragrant one-dish meals showcase meltingly tender meat, poultry, and seafood, served up with flavors from around the world. From Dubliner's Lamb Stew with Stout to New Orleans Hot Links with Red Beans and Rice, there's something here for everyone.

Perfect Pasta (and Risotto and Gnocchi and Grains . . .)

Pasta is one of the most delicious ways to get a meal on the table. When you have a bit of extra time, simmer up a pot of Rigatoni with Lamb Ragú, while No-Cook Spaghetti Puttanesca can be made in less time than it takes for the pasta water to boil.

Roasted and Grilled Suppers

Tossed together in a roasting pan or on the grill, these meat-and-vegetable dishes provide maximum taste with minimum effort. Seafood and poultry are represented by such dishes as Pesto Monkfish with Potatoes and Zucchini, and Roast Chicken with Mediterranean Vegetables.

Acknowledgments

Leslie and Rick would like to thank the following people for their help in creating this book, and for their constant support in our lives:

From Leslie

My husband and true love, Phillip

My darling daughter Rachel, and her husband, Bob

My soul mate, Marie Zazzi

From Rick

My irrepressible partner, Patrick Fisher

My irreplaceable friend, Diane Kniss

From Leslie and Rick

To everyone at John Wiley & Sons, including Natalie Chapman, Monique Calello, Brenda Blot, Gypsy Lovett, Pam Chirls, and Justin Schwartz, who were there when it really mattered

Our talented photographer, Duane Winfield

Our dear friend, Susan Wyler, with an extra helping of thanks

Our loyal and beloved agent, Susan Ginsburg

Introduction

If your life is anything like mine, it gets more complicated every day. For me, cooking is not only a profession but also a source of joy and accomplishment. When I get into the kitchen I want to relax, not be confronted with piles of ingredients and fancy techniques. I am a trained chef, and I know how to cook just about anything. But cooking at home is different from cooking in a restaurant, thank heavens.

My *The Simpler The Better* approach to cooking was born when I saw my busy daughter Rachel trying to raise her family and feed them well at the same time. I was challenged to develop some recipes to help her out. The concept was further refined when my dear friend Marie Zazzi shared her Italian approach to simple, incredibly flavorful cooking. The results were the first two books in this series. But these books were about the individual components of a meal: main course, side dish, dessert, and the occasional appetizer, soup, and salad.

I realized that my husband and I (joined by Rachel, her husband, and our darling grandsons Max and Henry as often as possible) very often sit down to a one-dish meal, sometimes filled out with a simple salad or bread. How often have I roasted a chicken or fish fillets along with a colorful assortment of vegetables to make our meal? Or filled bowls with a hearty soup or zesty pasta? Or arranged meat and vegetables on a platter to create a light, but filling main-course salad?

In this book, I turn my attention to those one-dish meals that I love to make so much, knowing that other cooks love them just as much as I do. Keeping in line with my theory that too many flavors and ingredients can muddle rather than improve a dish, I present recipes with an average of eight ingredients. Whenever possible, I cook all components of a dish in the same pot, skillet, or what-have-you to save on cleanup. As far as ingredients go, I restrict my grocery shopping to my local supermarket, with an occasional foray to a slightly more upscale natural foods market. I do not go traipsing all over town looking for special ingredients or resort to shopping online for exotica. What surprised me was the vast array of international ingredients available to the home cook, from Thai red curry paste and rice noodles to high-quality Italian Gorgonzola cheese. Please look in the supermarket for some of the groceries I've used that may be unfamiliar to you. I bet they're there . . . or at another market well within traveling distance.

I've learned to rely on certain groceries to add substance to my one-dish meals without any fuss. My pantry is stuffed with a selection of canned beans, pasta, rice, instant polenta, and chicken broth. My refrigerator always holds pesto, Dijon mustard, and pitted Kalamata olives. While I would never serve frozen vegetables as a side dish, they are great to have on hand for adding to casseroles and the like. I keep frozen corn, mixed vegetables (the familiar corn, carrot, and green bean combination), baby onions, and peas at the ready. My spice cabinet holds the usual assortment of jars, cans, and bottles, but I am never without certain spice blends, which add a mélange of seasonings to a dish with one shake. My favorites are Cajun and Italian seasonings, curry powder, and herbes de Provence. And, I must include my ever-trusty peppermill.

In many cases, I offer a complete meal in a single dish, mixing protein, vegetable, and a starchy component like potatoes or beans. However, in a world where so many people are watching their carbohydrate intake, often I give you the choice of whether to add a starchy side dish or not. And if your appetite requires, you might want to serve a green salad with a dish to round out a meal. In other words, there are options.

As in the first two books, there are three different ways for me to convey supplemental information about a recipe: In *Variations,* I show ways to make substitutions or simple methods for altering a dish; *Simple Tips* explain details on certain ingredients, cooking utensils, or techniques; and *Dress It Up* when you want to take the recipe one step further with garnishes or additional seasonings. In this book, I've added a *Prep* section. I find that it's very helpful to have the food ready (peeled, sliced, or otherwise prepared) before cooking actually starts, and I hope that this helps you keep organized, too.

A word on seasoning: I have not included salt and pepper in my ingredient count, as they are found in every kitchen and do not require being added to a shopping list. When I say "season to taste," it is for foods that you can actually put in your mouth and taste to evaluate the seasoning. If the food is unhealthful to consume raw (eggs or meat, for example), I have provided measured amounts of salt and pepper for seasoning, but you are free to use your own standards. By the way, I much prefer the coarse texture and clean flavor of kosher salt. If you use iodized or table salt, which has smaller crystals and therefore measures differently than kosher salt, please use about one-fourth less than my measurement.

When testing recipes for this book, I found myself turning to the same cooking utensils again and again. Their efficiency was so obvious that it just seemed silly to use anything else. For stews, ragùs, and other braised dishes, I reach for my 7-quart enameled cast-iron Dutch oven, which holds heat like a dream. For sautés and stir-fries, nothing beats a high-quality, heavy-gauge 12-inch skillet. In some cases, I used a smaller 9-inch skillet. In either case, it's important that the food cooks without crowding to allow even browning. (Crowded food creates steam that has nowhere to go, and steam inhibits browning.) When roasting, I find a heavy 18 x 13-inch roasting pan will hold meat and vegetables with room to spare.

Food does not have to be complicated to be delicious. I aim for no-frills, high-flavor cooking. I hope that this book makes your time in the kitchen simpler and better.

the simpler the better # Soup for Supper

Hot Beef Borscht

Here's a streamlined version of an old favorite. Most recipes for borscht have many ingredients that require plenty of chopping. Using pickled beets jettisons the tedious task of peeling and chopping raw beets. And packaged cole slaw saves prep time, too. This is a hot soup, chunky with beef cubes. For chilled vegetarian borscht, see the variation.

1¹/₄ pounds boneless beef chuck
1 medium onion
1 tablespoon vegetable oil, plus more as needed
One 14¹/₂-ounce can chopped tomatoes in juice
One 16-ounce jar pickled sliced beets
3 cups packaged cole slaw mix (¹/₂ of a 1-pound bag)

PREP *Cut beef into 1-inch chunks. Chop onion.*

1 Heat oil in soup pot over medium-high heat. Season beef with salt and pepper. Add beef and cook, turning beef occasionally, until browned, about 5 minutes. Transfer meat to plate. Add onion and cook, stirring often, until onion softens, about 3 minutes.

2 Return beef to pot. Add 4 cups water and tomatoes with juices and bring to a boil,

scraping up browned bits on bottom of pot. Reduce heat to medium-low and partially cover pot. Simmer until beef is almost tender, about 1 hour.

3 Stir in pickled beets with pickling juices and cole slaw mix. Cook until beef is very tender, about 20 minutes more. Season with salt and pepper. Remove from heat. Skim fat from surface of soup. Serve hot.

6 SERVINGS

other ideas

SIMPLE TIP *Buy pickled beets and not the plain canned variety. The former will be packed in a flavorful sweet-and-sour liquid, all the better to flavor the borscht.*

DRESS IT UP *For an herb flavor, stir 2 tablespoons chopped fresh dill into the soup just before serving.*

Don't resist: Top each serving with a dollop of sour cream.

VARIATION *Borscht with beef doesn't make good cold soup because the beef fat will harden when chilled. To make a vegetarian soup, delete the beef chuck. Cook 1 carrot and 2 celery stalks, both chopped into $1/2$-inch dice, with the onion and cook until the vegetables are softened, about 5 minutes. If you wish, add 2 medium boiling potatoes, scrubbed and cut into $1/2$-inch cubes. Instead of 4 cups water, use vegetable broth. Simmer the vegetables in the broth for about 1 hour before adding the beets and cole slaw mix. Cool the soup to room temperature, then cover and refrigerate until chilled, at least 4 hours.*

Butternut Squash and Pasta Soup

Butternut squash is often blended into a smooth pureed soup, but here the brightly colored cubes are left au naturel. Bits of meaty prosciutto and aromatic chopped fresh sage play off the sweetness of the squash in a very special way, and pasta provides ballast.

3 ounces (1/8 inch thick) sliced prosciutto

1 medium onion

1 tablespoon extra-virgin olive oil

1 butternut squash (about 1 1/2 pounds), peeled, seeded, and cut into 1-inch pieces (see *Simple Tip*)

Two 14 1/2-ounce cans chicken broth

2 tablespoons chopped fresh sage, or 2 teaspoons dried rubbed sage

1/3 cup ditalini or other small pasta for soup

Freshly grated Parmesan cheese, for serving

PREP *Chop prosciutto into 1/4-inch dice. Chop onion.*

1 Heat olive oil in soup pot over medium-high heat. Add prosciutto and cook, stirring occasionally, until prosciutto is beginning to brown, about 3 minutes. Add squash and onion, reduce heat to medium, and cover. Cook, stirring occasionally, until onion is translucent, about 5 minutes.

2 Stir in broth and 1 cup water and bring to a boil over high heat. Return heat to medium-low and simmer for 15 minutes.

3 Add sage and pasta and cook until squash and pasta are tender, about 12 minutes. Season with salt and pepper. Serve hot, with Parmesan cheese passed on the side.

4 TO 6 SERVINGS

other ideas

SIMPLE TIP *Some supermarkets now sell peeled and cubed butternut squash. If you want to use it, you'll need about 20 ounces instead of the whole butternut squash. To prepare it yourself, it is much easier to peel the entire squash than to cut and pare individual cubes. Here's how: Peel the squash with a sturdy vegetable peeler, pressing hard to reveal the orange flesh. Using a heavy knife, cut the squash lengthwise, and scoop out the seeds before cutting into cubes.*

DRESS IT UP *Leave out the sage and top each serving with a dollop of pesto.*

VARIATION *Instead of the sage, use 1 tablespoon chopped fresh rosemary or 1 1/2 teaspoons dried rosemary.*

Red Curry Chicken and Rice Soup

With the increasing popularity of Thai cooking, supermarkets are stocking more Asian products. Here, good old chicken and rice soup gets a makeover with the exotic flavors of red curry paste and coconut milk.

2 boneless and skinless chicken breasts, about 14 ounces total

1 medium onion

2 medium carrots

2 tablespoons vegetable oil

One 13 $1/2$-ounce can coconut milk (do not stir or shake)

1 $1/2$ tablespoons Thai red curry paste

One 14 $1/2$-ounce can chicken broth

$1/3$ cup long-grain rice

PREP *Cut chicken into bite-size pieces. Chop onion. Cut carrots into $1/4$-inch-thick rounds.*

1 Heat 1 tablespoon oil in a soup pot over medium-high heat. Add chicken and cook, stirring occasionally, until chicken turns opaque, about 5 minutes. Do not brown chicken. Transfer chicken to a plate.

2 Heat remaining tablespoon oil in pot. Add onion and carrots, and cook until onion is translucent, about 5 minutes. Scoop $1/4$ cup of the thick coconut cream from top of coconut milk and add to pot. (If your brand of coconut does not have this thick

cream layer, just use coconut milk.) Add curry paste and stir for 30 seconds. Stir in remaining coconut milk and chicken broth, whisk well, and bring to a boil. Reduce heat to low and cover. Simmer for 15 minutes.

3 Add rice and cook for 10 minutes. Add chicken and cook until chicken is cooked through and rice is tender, about 10 minutes more. Season with salt. Serve hot.

4 TO 6 SERVINGS

other ideas

SIMPLE TIP *Red curry paste will be very reasonably priced at Asian grocers, but it can also be found at many supermarkets and natural food stores. Thai curry paste includes solid ingredients like shallots, lemongrass, and garlic in addition to spices and comes in red, green, or yellow varieties (the exact proportion of ingredients and spices contributes to the color). Store any leftover curry paste in a small covered container for up to a week. (Red Curry Beef with Potatoes on page 136 also uses red curry paste.) If you can't find it, use 1 tablespoon Madras-style curry powder, adding 2 finely chopped garlic cloves to the saucepan with the onion and carrots.*

DRESS IT UP *Green beans are a fine addition to this soup. During the last 5 minutes or so of cooking, add $1/4$ pound green beans, trimmed and cut into 1-inch pieces.*

Sprinkle each serving with chopped fresh cilantro or mint.

VARIATIONS *Make this with peeled, deveined shrimp. Delete the chicken and 1 tablespoon of oil in Step 1. Stir the raw shrimp into the soup in Step 3.*

Add 2 garlic cloves, finely chopped, to the pot after sautéing the onions and carrots.

Mexican Chicken Soup with Tortillas

Every country in the world must have its own favorite chicken soup, and this one represents the Mexican contingent. It's chunky with corn and pieces of chicken, with a crunchy topping of crumbled tortillas on each serving—think of them as Mexican croutons.

2 pounds chicken thighs

1 medium onion

1 tablespoon olive oil

One 14 $1/2$-ounce can diced tomatoes with chiles

One 14 $1/2$-ounce can chicken broth

2 cups fresh or frozen defrosted corn kernels

1 teaspoon dried oregano

Unsalted corn tortilla chips, for serving

PREP *Rinse chicken and pat dry. Chop onion into $1/2$-inch dice.*

1 Heat olive oil in soup pot over medium-high heat. Add chicken, skin side down, and cook until undersides are golden brown, about 5 minutes. Turn and brown the other side, about 5 minutes more. Transfer chicken to plate.

2 Pour out all but 1 tablespoon fat from pot. Return pot to stove and reduce heat to medium. Add onion and cook, stirring often, until onion softens, about 3 minutes. Return chicken to pot. Add tomatoes and chiles with juices, chicken broth, 1 cup

water, corn, and oregano. Bring to a boil over high heat. Reduce heat to low and partially cover pot. Simmer until chicken is cooked through, about 45 minutes.

3   Transfer chicken to cutting board. Cut meat into bite-size pieces, discarding skin and bones. Return meat to pot. Skim fat from surface of soup. Serve hot, topping each serving with a handful of tortilla chips.

4 TO 6 SERVINGS

other ideas

SIMPLE TIP *I am never without a bag of frozen yellow corn in the freezer. It is so easy to add the defrosted kernels to soups and casseroles (and even pasta, such as the All-American Carbonara with Corn, Bacon, and Jalapeño on page 170). To quickly defrost, measure out the corn and place it in a wire sieve. Rinse the corn under warm water for a minute or so. That's it.*

VARIATION *Spice it up by adding a minced jalapeño and 2 minced garlic cloves to the pot with the onion.*

Chicken and Tortellini Soup with Pesto

Crave a big bowl of chicken soup, but don't have the time for the lengthy simmering? Let this recipe come to the rescue. I supplement canned chicken broth with browned chicken thighs and vegetables, then finish it off with tortellini and pesto. You'll get long-cooked flavor with very little effort.

2 pounds chicken thighs

1 medium onion

1 large carrot

1 large zucchini

1 tablespoon vegetable oil

One 48-ounce can chicken broth

$1/2$ pound frozen cheese-filled tortellini

2 tablespoons store-bought pesto

PREP *Rinse chicken and pat dry. Chop onion into $1/2$-inch dice. Chop carrot into $1/2$-inch dice. Cut zucchini lengthwise, then crosswise into $1/2$-inch-thick slices.*

1 Heat oil in soup pot over medium-high heat. Add chicken, skin side down, and cook until undersides are golden brown, about 5 minutes. Turn and brown the other side, about 5 minutes more. Transfer chicken to plate.

2 Pour out all but 1 tablespoon fat from pot. Return pot to stove and reduce heat to medium. Add onion and carrot and cook, stirring often, until onion softens, about 3 minutes. Add zucchini and cook until onion is translucent, about 3 minutes more. Return chicken to pot. Add broth and 1 cup water. Bring to a boil over high heat. Reduce heat to low and partially cover pot. Simmer until chicken is cooked through, about 45 minutes.

3 Transfer chicken to cutting board. Cut meat into bite-size pieces, discarding skin and bones. Return meat to pot and add tortellini. Return to a boil over high heat. Cook until tortellini is tender, about 10 minutes. Remove from heat. Skim fat from surface of soup. Stir in pesto. Serve hot.

6 SERVINGS

other ideas

SIMPLE TIP *All canned chicken broth is not created equal. There are very tasty brands, and then there are, well, not-so-tasty brands. Reduced-sodium broth has more natural flavor because the taste isn't hidden by salt, but watch out for the "salt-free" versions, which are often very bland.*

DRESS IT UP *Top each serving with a generous sprinkle of freshly grated Parmesan or domestic Asiago cheese.*

VARIATION *You can use turkey thighs instead of the chicken, but they will need to simmer for about 1 3/4 hours to become tender.*

Cod and Corn Chowder

A piping hot, creamy chowder has got to be one of the most satisfying things that you can ladle out of a soup pot. True, many chowders are based on shellfish, but meaty fish fillets, such as the cod in this recipe, can also get into the act. If you can, do make this with lemon thyme, as its citrus fragrance will make this an extraordinary soup.

1 medium onion

4 medium red-skinned potatoes, scrubbed but unpeeled

1 pound cod fillets

4 bacon strips

Two 8-ounce bottles clam juice

2 cups half-and-half

1 teaspoon chopped fresh thyme, or $1/2$ teaspoon dried

2 cups fresh or defrosted frozen corn kernels

PREP *Chop onion. Cut potatoes into $3/4$-inch pieces. Cut cod into 1-inch pieces.*

1   Place bacon in soup pot and cook over medium heat, turning once, until crisp and browned, about 6 minutes. Transfer to paper towels, leaving fat in pot. Cool and chop bacon.

2   Add onion to pot and cook, stirring occasionally, until onion softens, about 3 minutes. Add potatoes and cook until onion is translucent, about 3 minutes more. Add 1

cup water, clam juice, half-and-half, and thyme. Bring to a boil over high heat. Reduce heat to low and partially cover pot. Simmer until potatoes are tender, about 20 minutes.

3 Stir in cod and corn. Cook until cod is cooked through, about 6 minutes. Season with salt and pepper. Serve hot, sprinkling each serving with chopped bacon.

6 SERVINGS

other ideas

SIMPLE TIP *Even the most conscientious fishmonger may leave a few bones in the cod fillets. Run your fingers over both sides of the fillets to feel for any stray bones. If you find some, pluck them out with tweezers or sharp-nosed pliers. Because I cook a lot of fish, I reserve a pair of drugstore tweezers for removing fish bones, and you may want to follow suit. You will even find tweezers specifically made for the task at well-stocked kitchenware shops.*

DRESS IT UP *Top each serving with a dollop of red, black, or golden American caviar. Don't use artificially dyed black caviar, as the dye will bleed into the soup.*

VARIATION *If you want to use another kind of fish, stick to firm-fleshed varieties such as snapper and grouper.*

Provençal Fish Soup

All over the south of France, you'll find versions of this lovely soup. It is wonderful in its unadorned state, but French cooks often gild the lily. I've given instructions on one of the most popular garnishes—toasted bread with a garlic mayonnaise known as aïoli—in the *Dress It Up* section. Or, sprinkle each serving with freshly grated Gruyère or Parmesan cheese, another popular embellishment.

1 medium onion

2 garlic cloves

1 pound skinless red snapper fillets

2 tablespoons extra-virgin olive oil, plus more for serving

2 teaspoons herbes de Provence (see *Simple Tip,* page 59), or $^1/_2$ teaspoon each basil, thyme, rosemary, and oregano

One 28-ounce can chopped tomatoes in juice

One 8-ounce bottle clam juice

$^1/_3$ cup orzo (rice-shaped pasta)

PREP *Chop onion. Finely chop garlic. Cut fish into 1-inch pieces.*

1 Heat olive oil in soup pot over medium heat. Add onion and cook, stirring often, until onion is golden, about 5 minutes. Stir in garlic and cook until it gives off its aroma, about 1 minute. Stir in herbes de Provence.

2   Add 1 cup water, tomatoes with their juice, and clam juice. Bring to a boil over high heat. Reduce heat to medium-low and partially cover pot. Simmer for 30 minutes. Stir in orzo and cook until almost tender, about 12 minutes.

3   Stir in fish and cook until cooked through, about 5 minutes. Season with salt and pepper. Serve hot, providing a cruet of olive oil for drizzling over the soup.

6 SERVINGS

other ideas

SIMPLE TIP *If the fishmonger hasn't removed the skin from the fillets, you can do it yourself. Slip a sharp thin-bladed knife just under the flesh at the pointed end of the fillet to release a bit of the skin. Using a paper towel, grip the skin. Slide the knife along the length of the fillet, just where the skin meets the flesh, pulling on the skin at the same time to provide traction. The skin will come right off.*

DRESS IT UP *Add $1/2$ cup dry white wine or dry vermouth to the soup with the tomatoes.*

To make aïoli, mix $1/2$ cup mayonnaise with 2 garlic cloves crushed through a press. Toast slices of crusty bread. Top each serving of soup with a slice of bread and big dollop of aïoli.

VARIATION *For a bit more of that Provençal flavor, cook $1/2$ cup chopped fennel bulb with the onion. And, if you have it handy, add $1/4$ teaspoon crumbled saffron threads with the fish to the soup.*

Lentil Soup with Pasta and Rosemary

This is our old friend *pasta e fagioli.* It is usually called "pasta fazool" by Italian Americans whose appreciation for tasty and hearty soups isn't hampered by correct pronunciation. The elemental, earthy flavor of lentils is brightened by the bracing taste of fresh rosemary. If ever a soup was made for wiping the bowl with crusty bread, this is it.

$3/4$ pound smoked ham

1 medium onion

2 celery stalks with leaves

2 garlic cloves

1 tablespoon extra-virgin olive oil, plus more for serving

1 cup lentils, sorted for stones, rinsed, and drained

1 tablespoon chopped fresh rosemary, or 1 teaspoon crumbled dried

$1/2$ cup ditalini pasta

PREP *Cut ham into $1/2$-inch dice. Chop onion into $1/2$-dice. Chop celery into $1/2$-inch dice; coarsely chop leaves. Finely chop garlic.*

1 Heat olive oil in soup pot over medium heat. Add ham and cook, stirring occasionally, until lightly browned, about 5 minutes. Add onion and celery and cook, stirring occasionally, until onion is translucent, about 5 minutes. Add garlic and cook until it gives off its aroma, about 1 minute.

2 Add 4 cups water, lentils, and rosemary to pot. Bring to a boil over high heat. Reduce heat to low and partially cover pot. Simmer until lentils are barely tender, about 40 minutes.

3 Add ditalini and cook until pasta is tender, about 10 minutes. Season with salt and pepper. Serve hot, with a cruet of olive oil for drizzling over the soup.

4 SERVINGS

other ideas

SIMPLE TIP *When a recipe calls for smoked ham, look at the delicatessen counter for reliable examples of this tasty meat. Pass over versions that are pressed or glazed in favor of Black Forest ham or simply baked ham on the bone. Or, head over to the meat department and buy a ham steak, which is a big, vacuum-packed slab of ham. Cut the meat off the round bone as needed, and drop the bone into the soup for extra flavor (just don't forget to fish it out before serving).*

VARIATION *The combination of ham and vegetables provides plenty of flavor for the soup. However, for a somewhat richer version, you can substitute 2 cups canned chicken broth for an equal amount of the water.*

Smoke and Spice Mussel Chowder

This is a kind of Manhattan-style (that is, tomato-based) mussel chowder, but jalapeños and bacon give it a nice kick. Look for bacon that touts its smokiness on the label. The acid in the tomatoes slows the cooking of the potatoes, so it's important to boil the potatoes as the first step to save time.

1 medium onion

1 garlic clove

12 ounces Yukon Gold or red-skinned potatoes, scrubbed but unpeeled

2 pounds mussels

4 deeply smoked bacon strips, cut into 1-inch lengths

Two 14 1/2-ounce cans diced tomatoes with jalapeños

PREP *Chop onion. Finely chop garlic. Cut potatoes crosswise into 1/4-inch-thick rounds. If mussels have tough beards connected to their shells, snip beards off with scissors.*

1   Place potatoes in a pot and add enough lightly salted cold water to barely cover potatoes. Bring to a boil over high heat. Reduce heat to medium and cover. Cook until potatoes are just tender, about 15 minutes. Do not overcook, as they will cook again. Drain and set aside.

2   Dry pot and place over medium heat. Add bacon and cook, occasionally turning bacon, until crisp and brown, about 6 minutes. Use a slotted spoon to transfer bacon

to paper towels; cool and coarsely chop bacon. Add onion and garlic to pot and cook, stirring occasionally, until onion softens, about 3 minutes. Stir in tomatoes and jalapeños with their juice and $1/2$ cup water. Bring to a boil. Reduce heat to medium-low and cover pot. Simmer for 20 minutes.

3 Add mussels and potatoes and increase the heat to high. Cook, occasionally shaking the pot, until mussels have opened, about 5 minutes. Discard any mussels that do not open. Season with salt and pepper. Serve hot, in large deep soup bowls, topped with chopped bacon.

4 SERVINGS

other ideas

SIMPLE TIP *Mussels harvested from the ocean are delicious, but they must be well scrubbed under cold water to remove surface grit. Also, the beards (the tough cords the mussels use to attach themselves to rocks) must be removed. Farm-raised mussels are already cleaned and debearded, making them great time-savers.*

DRESS IT UP *Scatter some chopped cilantro over each serving.*

For even more heat and smoke, substitute plain diced tomatoes for the ones with jalapeños. Add 1 canned chipotle chile in adobo sauce, finely chopped, along with any sauce that clings to the chile.

VARIATION *Of course, littleneck clams are good this way, too. Scrub them well under cold water before using.*

Pinto Bean Soup with Chorizo and Sherry

Start with dried beans to make bean soup, and it's a fairly lengthy proposition. Even though my streamlined version uses canned beans, it still has a lovely Spanish flavor profile, thanks to the chorizo and sherry.

3 ounces smoked chorizo links

1 medium onion

2 garlic cloves

Three 15- to 19-ounce cans pinto beans, drained and rinsed

One 14$^1/_2$-ounce can chicken broth

$^1/_3$ cup dry sherry

PREP *Cut chorizo into $^1/_2$-inch pieces. Chop onion. Finely chop garlic.*

1 Combine chorizo and $^1/_4$ cup water in medium saucepan. Cook over medium heat, stirring often, until water evaporates and chorizo is sizzling in fat, about 5 minutes. Add onion and garlic and cook until onion softens, about 5 minutes.

2 Add beans, broth, sherry, and 1 cup water and bring to a boil. Reduce heat to medium-low and partially cover pot. Simmer until well flavored, about 30 minutes.

3 Remove saucepan from heat. Using a large spoon, crush some beans against side of saucepan to thicken soup as desired. Season with salt and pepper. Serve hot.

6 SERVINGS

SIMPLE TIP *As unlikely as it sounds, there are almost the same amount of beans in a drained 15 1/2-ounce can as there are in a 19-ounce can. However, the quality of the beans varies from brand to brand. Latino brands are a reliable source of plump, unbroken canned beans.*

DRESS IT UP *Top each serving with shredded pepper jack cheese.*

VARIATION *Chile lovers may add 1 jalapeño, seeded and finely chopped, to the saucepan with the onion and garlic.*

Italian Sausage Soup

Because sausage is seasoned with herbs and salt, it can quickly turn a pot of water into soup. Well, maybe you'll need a few other ingredients, too. How about onion, celery, and garlic? Don't forget the Parmesan cheese, and maybe a slice of toasted bread to add a bit more substance. But that's all.

4 medium celery stalks with leaves

1 medium onion

2 garlic cloves

4 slices crusty, rustic-style bread

1 tablespoon extra-virgin olive oil

1 pound sweet or hot Italian sausage, casings removed

Freshly grated Parmesan cheese, for serving

PREP *Chop celery. Chop onion. Finely chop garlic. Toast bread slices.*

1 Heat olive oil in a large saucepan over medium-high heat. Add sausage and cook, breaking up sausage into bite-size pieces with the side of a spoon, until the sausage is browned, about 10 minutes. Use a slotted spoon to transfer sausage to a plate. Pour out all but 1 tablespoon of fat from pot.

2 Return pot to medium heat. Add celery, onion, and garlic. Cook, stirring occasionally,

until onion is translucent, about 5 minutes. Return sausage to pot and add 4 cups cold water. Bring to a boil over high heat. Partially cover saucepan with a lid. Reduce heat to medium-low and simmer for 30 minutes. Season with salt and pepper.

3 To serve, place a toasted bread slice in each soup bowl. Ladle soup over bread and serve immediately, with Parmesan passed on the side.

4 TO 6 SERVINGS

other ideas

SIMPLE TIP *To remove the pork sausage casings, use kitchen scissors to snip a slit up the side of each sausage. The loosened casing will be easy to peel off.*

DRESS IT UP *Add 4 cups well-washed, thinly sliced kale to the soup along with the water and sausage.*

In addition to (or in place of) the kale, add one 15- to 19-ounce can drained and rinsed white kidney (cannellini) beans.

Sprinkle each serving with thinly sliced fresh basil leaves.

VARIATION *Use turkey sausage instead of pork, if you wish.*

Creamy Turkey Soup with Celery Dumplings

Old-fashioned in all the best ways, this is the kind of soup from which legends are made. One taste will conjure up the image of an American Mom in a ruffled gingham apron. The soup starts out as a broth, but becomes creamy when the dumplings are added.

1 large onion

2 medium carrots

2 medium celery stalks with leaves

1 tablespoon vegetable oil

1 turkey breast with skin and bone, about 2 $1/4$ pounds

1 teaspoon poultry seasoning, or $1/4$ teaspoon each dried thyme, sage, rosemary, and marjoram

2 cups Easy Baking Mix (page 26), or use store-bought biscuit mix

$2/3$ cup milk

PREP *Chop onion into $1/2$-inch dice. Cut carrots into $1/2$-inch dice. Cut celery into $1/2$-inch dice; chop leaves finely—you will need $1^1/2$ tablespoons.*

1 Heat oil in soup pot over medium heat. Add turkey breast, skin side down, and cook until skin is golden brown, about 5 minutes. Remove from pot. Pour out all but 1 tablespoon fat from pot. Return to medium heat and add onion, carrots, and celery. Cook, stirring often, until vegetables soften, about 5 minutes.

2   Return turkey to pot and add 6 cups water. Bring to a boil, skimming off foam that rises to surface. Stir in poultry seasoning. Reduce heat to medium-low and simmer until thermometer inserted in thickest part of turkey reads 165°F, about 50 minutes. Transfer turkey to cutting board. Cut meat into bite-size chunks, discarding skin and bones. Return meat to soup.

3   Mix biscuit mix, milk, and chopped celery leaves in medium bowl to make sticky dough. Drop by scant tablespoons into simmering soup to make 12 dumplings. Simmer uncovered for 10 minutes. Cover tightly and cook until dumplings are cooked through, about 10 minutes more. Serve hot.

6 SERVINGS

other ideas

SIMPLE TIP *Some cooks habitually discard celery tops. True, too many celery leaves can make a dish bitter. However, when handled with restraint, they add a nice, herbaceous flavor to broths and soups.*

DRESS IT UP *For a richer soup, add $1/3$ cup heavy cream to the broth before adding the dumplings.*

VARIATION *Many fresh herbs can be substituted for the celery leaves—tarragon, parsley, and dill are just a few. If you use rosemary or sage, which can be strong, reduce the amount to 2 teaspoons.*

Easy Baking Mix

Most baby boomers grew up with a box of baking mix in the kitchen cabinet, ready and waiting to go into action for a wide range of baked goods and more. It's so easy to make your own that I never buy it. Here's my recipe, but you are free to use store-bought mix if you prefer. I use it most often to make dumplings for stews and soups (see previous recipe), but it makes a batch of biscuits in a flash. And it is there for the times when all I want for breakfast (or supper) is a stack of pancakes.

> 6 cups all-purpose flour
> 3 tablespoons baking powder
> 1 tablespoon salt
> 1 ^{1}/$_4$ cups chilled vegetable shortening, or 2 ^{1}/$_2$ sticks unsalted butter, thinly
>   sliced (see *Simple Tip*)

1   Whisk flour, baking powder, and salt in a large bowl. Add shortening. Using pastry blender, cut shortening into flour until mixture resembles coarse crumbs. Transfer to an airtight container and store in the refrigerator for up to 6 months (1 month if using butter).

MAKES ABOUT 7 ^{1}/$_2$ CUPS

SIMPLE TIP *Shortening makes the lightest biscuits and dumplings, but butter has the best flavor. If you wish, use 10 tablespoons each shortening and butter.*

EASY BISCUITS *Mix 2 cups baking mix with $^2/_3$ cup milk, knead gently in bowl a few times, and pat out on floured work surface into a 6-inch square about $^1/_2$-inch thick. Cut into 9 squares (you won't have any waste, as opposed to round biscuits, where the scraps must be rekneaded). Place on ungreased baking sheet and bake at 400°F until golden brown, about 12 minutes.*

MAKES 9 BISCUITS.

EASY PANCAKES *Whisk 2 cups biscuit mix, $^1/_4$ cup milk, 2 beaten large eggs, and 2 tablespoons sugar in a medium bowl just until barely smooth with a few lumps. Heat a griddle over high heat until water splashed on the surface instantly forms bouncing balls. Grease griddle. Pour $^1/_3$ cup batter onto griddle for each pancake. Cook until bubbles form on surface on pancake, about 2 minutes. Turn and cook to brown reverse side, about 1 minute more. Serve hot with butter and maple syrup.*

MAKES ABOUT 9 PANCAKES.

the simpler the better # Salad

for Dinner

Antipasto Pasta Salad

You can make this salad from bits and pieces of leftover goodies, or make a quick stop at the Italian deli on the way home and pick up what you need. Substituting whatever you have on hand for one ingredient or another is not only allowed but encouraged.

1 1/2 jarred roasted red peppers, drained

1/2 cup pitted and coarsely chopped Kalamata olives

One 6-ounce jar marinated artichoke hearts, drained

3 ounces sliced salami

3 ounces sliced provolone

1/2 pound shell-shaped pasta

1 1/2 tablespoons red wine vinegar

1/3 cup extra-virgin olive oil

PREP *Coarsely chop red peppers, olives, artichoke hearts, salami, and provolone.*

1 Bring large pot of lightly salted water to a boil over high heat. Add pasta and cook until tender, about 8 minutes. Drain and rinse under cold water.

2 Whisk vinegar, 1/4 teaspoon salt, and 1/4 teaspoon freshly ground pepper to dissolve salt in medium bowl. Gradually whisk in olive oil.

3 Add peppers, olives, artichoke hearts, salami, and cheese and mix well. Serve at room temperature.

4 SERVINGS

other ideas

SIMPLE TIP *Look for whole red peppers in jars. Imported brands are often very good, but read the labels and pass over those that use citric acid, which adds an odd flavor to the peppers.*

DRESS IT UP *Add 2 tablespoons chopped fresh basil, parsley, or oregano (or a combination) to the salad.*

VARIATIONS *Substitute mozzarella cheese for the provolone.*

Substitute soppressata for the salami.

Substitute 1 cup drained and coarsely chopped pickled Italian vegetables (giardinara) for the red peppers and artichokes.

Smoked Chicken, Apple, and Gruyère Salad with Toasted Walnuts

Most upscale supermarkets now carry smoked chicken breast, which is as delicious as it is versatile. The nutty flavor of the Gruyère cheese is played up with chopped walnuts and played against with tart apples. I don't blame you for thinking that you might skip toasting the walnuts, but please try to make the time—it does make a difference.

2 smoked chicken breasts, about $1\frac{1}{4}$ pounds total

1 bunch watercress, about 7 ounces

$\frac{1}{2}$ cup walnuts

2 Granny Smith apples

2 tablespoons sherry or cider vinegar

$1\frac{1}{3}$ cups shredded Gruyère cheese, about 5 ounces

$\frac{1}{2}$ cup walnut or vegetable oil

PREP *Remove skin from chicken breasts. Chop breasts into bite-size pieces. Remove tough stems from watercress. Coarsely chop watercress.*

1 Preheat oven to 350°F. Spread walnuts on baking sheet. Bake, stirring occasionally, until walnuts are lightly toasted and fragrant, about 10 minutes. Cool. Coarsely chop walnuts.

2   Peel, core, and chop apples into $1/2$-inch dice. Whisk vinegar, $1/4$ teaspoon salt, and $1/8$ teaspoon pepper in medium bowl. Add apples to bowl and toss.

3   Add chicken, watercress, walnuts, and cheese to bowl and toss. Add walnut oil and toss well. Season with salt and pepper. Serve immediately.

4 SERVINGS

other ideas

SIMPLE TIP *The most flavorful walnut oil is imported from France. Available at specialty food stores and many supermarkets, it can be pricey, but its distinctive flavor makes it a worthwhile purchase. It should be refrigerated because it could easily go rancid in a couple of months if stored at room temperature.*

VARIATION *Instead of store-bought chicken, this salad is a great way to use leftover grilled chicken or turkey, especially if it has picked up smoky flavor from the barbecue grill.*

Chopped Cobb Salad with Roquefort Dressing

Here are the basic elements of the famous Cobb salad, put together in a slightly different way. Instead of crumbled blue cheese as a component, why not make a thick, tangy Roquefort dressing to top each serving? Use leftover roasted chicken breast or meat from a super-market rotisserie bird.

$1/2$ cup sour cream

$1/2$ cup mayonnaise

2 teaspoons red wine vinegar

$1/2$ cup (2 ounces) crumbled Roquefort cheese

1 romaine lettuce heart, about $5 1/2$ ounces

2 cups bite-size roasted chicken, about 10 ounces

$1/2$ pint grape tomatoes

2 ripe avocados, pitted, peeled, and cut into $3/4$-inch dice (see *Simple Tip*)

1 Stir sour cream, mayonnaise, and vinegar together in bowl with rubber spatula. Add Roquefort and mix, mashing about half of Roquefort into mayonnaise mixture.

2 Cut romaine heart crosswise into $1/2$-inch-wide strips; discard lettuce core. Rinse and dry lettuce strips. Place in bowl with chicken, tomatoes, and avocados.

3   Serve, with the Roquefort dressing passed on the side.

4 SERVINGS

other ideas

SIMPLE TIP *To peel an avocado, first be sure it is ripe; it should give to slight pressure when squeezed. Cut the avocado in half lengthwise, through the stem end, all the way around. Twist apart the 2 halves, and the pit will remain in one half. Whack the pit with the sharp edge of a sharp knife—the blade should stick in the pit. Twist the knife to lift out the pit, pluck it off the blade, and discard it. Use a large metal serving spoon to scoop the avocado flesh in one piece from of each half; discard the peel.*

DRESS IT UP *Sprinkle each serving with crumbled cooked bacon.*

VARIATION *Roquefort is my favorite blue cheese, but Gorgonzola or Danish blue cheese are also options.*

Ham, Green Bean, and Potato Salad

the simpler the better

This hearty salad can be served warm, which is a good thing because you may not have the patience to wait for it to cool. Cooled completely, it is a great candidate for a filling salad to carry to a picnic or potluck.

One 28-ounce bag small red-skinned or Yukon Gold potatoes
(about 28 potatoes)
10 ounces green beans
2 tablespoons white wine vinegar
1 $1/2$ teaspoons Dijon mustard
$1/2$ cup extra-virgin olive oil
$1/2$ pound smoked ham
1 scallion
2 tablespoons chopped fresh parsley

PREP *Scrub potatoes, but do not peel. Trim green beans and cut into 1-inch lengths. Cut ham into bite-size cubes. Thinly slice white and green parts of scallion.*

1 Bring large saucepan of lightly salted water to a boil over high heat. Add potatoes and cook until almost tender when pierced with tip of a small knife, about 12 minutes. Add green beans and cook until potatoes and beans are tender, about 5 minutes more. Drain and rinse under cold water to stop cooking.

2 Whisk vinegar, mustard, $1/4$ teaspoon salt, and $1/8$ teaspoon pepper in medium bowl. Gradually whisk in olive oil.

3 Cut potatoes in half and add to bowl. Toss, add green beans, ham, scallions, and parsley, and toss again. Serve warm, cooled to room temperature, or chilled.

4 SERVINGS

other ideas

SIMPLE TIP *Peeling brown-skinned potatoes for potato salad can be quite a chore, especially if making salad for a crowd. The answer is to use Yukon Gold, red bliss, or other varieties with thin, edible skins. Just give them a good scrubbing before cooking.*

DRESS IT UP *Stir $1/3$ cup crème fraîche or sour cream into the salad.*

VARIATION *Make the salad with chopped dill instead of parsley.*

Pizza Panzarella

Bread salad, such as this Italian *panzarella,* is more than a way to use stale bread—it's very tasty, too. The bread must be rustic style, with a crisp crust and a tight crumb, for anything with less body will make a very soggy, unappetizing salad. The typical flavors of pizza (tomatoes, basil, and mozzarella) blend beautifully with the bread.

$1/2$ pound firm, day-old, crusty rustic-style bread

4 ripe plum tomatoes

$1/4$ pound mozzarella, preferably fresh mozzarella

$1\,1/2$ tablespoons red wine vinegar

1 garlic clove, crushed through a press

$1/3$ cup plus 1 tablespoon extra-virgin olive oil

$1/2$ cup packed coarsely chopped basil leaves

PREP *Tear bread into bite-size pieces, about 1 inch square. You should have about 4 cups. Cut tomatoes into $1/2$-inch dice. Cut mozzarella into $1/2$-inch dice.*

1 Place bread in medium bowl and sprinkle with about 1 cup water to moisten thoroughly. Let stand 1 minute. Squeeze bread to remove excess water.

2 Whisk vinegar and garlic with $1/2$ teaspoon salt and $1/4$ teaspoon pepper in medium bowl. Gradually whisk in olive oil. Add soaked bread.

3 Add tomatoes, mozzarella, and basil and toss well. Season with salt and pepper. Serve immediately.

4 SERVINGS

other ideas

SIMPLE TIP *The bread should be only a day or two old—just old enough to be firm but not so old as to have acquired off flavors. If you want to make the salad but have doubts that the bread is firm enough, you can bake the bread to dry it out. Spread the bite-size bread pieces on a baking sheet and bake in a preheated 400°F oven until the edges of bread begin to crisp. Remove from the oven and cool completely. The bread will become firmer as it cools.*

DRESS IT UP *Anything that you like on your pizza will go well in this salad. Add thin strips of salami or pepperoni, chopped roasted red peppers, chopped pitted olives, or minced anchovy fillets.*

Rice Salad with Shrimp, Peas, and Rosemary

Rice makes as fine a salad as pasta or potatoes, but the cook must keep one caveat in mind. Never serve rice salad chilled, as the starches in rice turn unpleasantly hard when refrigerated. However, it will soften again at room temperature.

If you want to make this salad ahead, refrigerate the dressed salad without the shrimp. Remove the salad from the refrigerator an hour before serving, to lose its chill and soften, then stir in the cold shrimp.

1 pound large (21–25 count) shrimp

1 cup long-grain rice

1 1/2 tablespoons freshly squeezed lemon juice

1/3 cup extra-virgin olive oil

1 tablespoon chopped fresh rosemary

1 cup defrosted frozen peas

PREP *Peel and devein shrimp (or purchase them already cleaned).*

Bring large saucepan of lightly salted water to a boil over high heat. Add shrimp and cook just until they turn opaque, about 3 minutes. Using skimmer or wire strainer, transfer shrimp to bowl of ice water to cool.

2 Add rice to shrimp cooking water and cook until tender, about 18 minutes. Drain in wire strainer; rinse under cold water to cool. Drain well.

3 Whisk lemon juice, $1/4$ teaspoon salt, and $1/4$ teaspoon pepper in medium bowl. Gradually whisk in olive oil. Drain shrimp and add to bowl. Add rice, rosemary, and peas and mix well. Season with salt and pepper and serve.

4 TO 6 SERVINGS

other ideas

SIMPLE TIP *Look for "easy peel" shrimp that have already been deveined, making it a simple task to pull off the shell and tail. Check to be sure that the shrimp have been deveined. If not, use the tip of a small sharp knife to remove the veins, working under a stream of cold running water. Nude shrimp that have been peeled and deveined are available, but they are expensive and not as flavorful as the easy-peel variety.*

DRESS IT UP *Substitute sugar snap peas for the frozen peas. Pull back each pod at the stem end to remove the string. Before cooking the shrimp, cook the sugar snap peas in the boiling water just until they turn a brighter shade of green, about $1^1/2$ minutes. Using a skimmer or a wire strainer, transfer the sugar snap peas to a bowl of ice water to cool. Drain before using.*

Warm Salmon, Asparagus, and Scallion Salad

This chunky salad needs no greens, although you could serve it on top of a handful of mesclun, if you like. It has a kind of simplicity that is reminiscent of certain Asian dishes, even though its flavors are firmly in the French realm.

1 lemon
1 pound asparagus
1 scallion
3 tablespoons extra-virgin olive oil
1 1/2 pounds skinless salmon fillet, cut into 2 or 3 pieces to fit the skillet
1 tablespoon chopped fresh tarragon

PREP *Grate zest from lemon. Squeeze juice from lemon; you should have 1 1/2 table-spoons juice. Snap woody ends from asparagus. Cut spears into 1 1/2-inch lengths. Thinly slice white and green parts of scallion.*

1 Whisk lemon zest and juice with 1/2 teaspoon salt and 1/4 teaspoon pepper in a medium bowl. Gradually whisk in olive oil; set the vinaigrette aside.

2 Fill large skillet half full with lightly salted water and bring to a boil over high heat. Arrange asparagus in a single layer in skillet and cover. Reduce heat to medium and cook asparagus until crisp-tender, about 4 minutes, depending on thickness of asparagus. Using slotted spatula, transfer asparagus to colander. Add salmon to water

and reduce heat to medium-low. Simmer until salmon is just opaque when flaked with tip of a knife, about 10 minutes. Using slotted spatula, transfer salmon to bowl with vinaigrette.

3 Using a fork, break salmon into bite-size pieces. Add asparagus, scallion, and tarragon, and mix gently to combine. Season with salt and a few grinds of black pepper. Serve warm.

4 SERVINGS

other ideas

SIMPLE TIP *Don't forget to grate the zest from citrus (in this case, the lemon) before squeezing the juice. Actually, with the new very fine zesters on the market, forgetting to do so isn't the disaster it used to be. Regardless, when writing a recipe, I always put the lemon zest before the lemon juice, just as a helpful reminder.*

DRESS IT UP *Top each serving with crisply cooked crumbled bacon.*

Use a combination of 1 teaspoon each finely chopped fresh tarragon, parsley, and chives instead of just tarragon.

If you would like to serve the salad on greens, they should be also dressed with lemon vinaigrette. Make a double batch of the lemon dressing; pour half of the dressing into another medium bowl. Add 4 cups mixed greens, such as mesclun, and toss well. Serve equal amounts of the greens in bowls, and divide the salmon salad among the bowls.

VARIATION *Instead of the asparagus, use 6 ounces sugar snap peas. They will take only 2 or 3 minutes to cook to crisp-tender. Substitute fresh dill for the tarragon.*

Warm Sea Scallop Salad with Lemon-Basil Couscous

This restaurant-style dish gives sophisticated results with little effort. The only thing to watch out for is timing—while the scallops roast, make the couscous. The couscous is very forgiving, and if it needs to wait an extra few minutes, don't worry. Or make the couscous salad ahead and serve it chilled or at room temperature next to the seared scallops.

12 sea scallops, about 1 $1/4$ pounds total

1 cup frozen peas

2 lemons

$1/2$ cup plus 2 tablespoons extra-virgin olive oil

1 $1/3$ cups couscous

$1/4$ cup packed thinly sliced basil

PREP *If attached, peel off and discard tiny side muscles from scallops. Defrost peas by placing peas in wire strainer and rinsing under warm water. Grate zest from 1 lemon. Squeeze juice from lemons; you should have 3 tablespoons juice.*

1 Position oven rack in top third of oven and thoroughly preheat oven to 450°F (this will take 20 minutes with most ovens). Place heavy, 12-inch ovenproof skillet in oven

until the skillet is very hot, about 5 minutes. Toss scallops with 1 tablespoon olive oil. Remove skillet from oven and place scallops flat in skillet—do not crowd scallops in pan. Roast scallops until bottoms brown, about 5 minutes. Turn and roast 1 minute more.

2   Meanwhile, bring 1³/₄ cups water, 1 tablespoon olive oil, and ¹/₂ teaspoon salt in a medium saucepan to a boil over high heat. Stir in couscous and add peas. Cover tightly and remove from heat. Let stand until couscous has absorbed water and is tender, about 6 minutes.

3   Whisk lemon zest and juice with ¹/₄ teaspoon salt and ¹/₄ teaspoon pepper in small bowl. Gradually whisk in remaining ¹/₂ cup olive oil. Reserve 1 ¹/₂ tablespoons vinaigrette. Stir basil and remaining vinaigrette into couscous; season with salt and pepper. Spoon equal amounts of couscous on 4 dinner plates. Place scallops next to couscous and drizzle with reserved vinaigrette. Serve hot.

4 SERVINGS

other ideas

SIMPLE TIP *Be sure to use a large, heavy skillet for oven-roasting the scallops. If they are crowded, the scallops will steam and not brown properly. The pan should be 12 to 14 inches in diameter and ovenproof. My favorite skillets in this style are cast iron or heavy-duty, stainless steel–lined aluminum. They will become workhorses in your kitchen.*

DRESS IT UP *Chop a little extra basil to sprinkle on top of the scallops.*

VARIATION *Large (21–25 count) peeled and deveined shrimp can be oven-roasted in the same manner.*

Spinach Greek Salad with Pita Toasts

Serve this salad when a light meal is in order. Of course, you can beef it up with sliced cooked chicken breast or shrimp, if you wish, but there is something comforting about this popular mix of fresh greens, crisp cucumbers, and tart-sweet tomatoes, all accented with sharp feta cheese and crunchy pita toasts.

One 7-ounce bag baby spinach

1 large cucumber (but not the long seedless type)

3 ripe plum tomatoes

$1/2$ cup pitted Kalamata olives

3 ounces feta cheese

2 "pocket-style" pita breads

$1/2$ cup plus 2 tablespoons extra-virgin olive oil

2 tablespoons freshly squeezed lemon juice

PREP *Wash and spin spinach dry. Peel and slice cucumber. Slice tomatoes. Coarsely chop olives. Crumble feta cheese.*

1 Preheat oven to 400°F. Split pita breads crosswise with serrated knife and cut into eighths. Spread on baking sheet, cut sides up, and brush with 2 tablespoons olive oil. Bake until golden brown and crisp, about 10 minutes.

2 Whisk lemon juice, $1/2$ teaspoon salt, and $1/4$ teaspoon freshly ground pepper in large bowl. Gradually whisk in remaining $1/2$ cup olive oil.

3 Add spinach, cucumber, tomatoes, olives, and feta. Toss and serve with pita toasts.

4 SERVINGS

other ideas

SIMPLE TIP *For sautéing and general cooking, it's fine to use regular, golden-hued olive oil. But when the olive oil is served in a salad or another uncooked dish, green extra-virgin olive oil will have the best flavor. (However, because of its superior taste, I use moderately priced extra-virgin oil for cooking, too.)*

DRESS IT UP *Sprinkle the toasts with 2 tablespoons chopped fresh dill before baking.*

VARIATION *If you like anchovies, top the salad with a few fillets.*

Sliced Steak, Baby Spinach, and Roquefort Salad

Rather than ask you to fire up the grill (go ahead if you are in the mood), the tender, flavorful sirloin used here is pan-cooked in a heavy skillet. This method gives the meat a nicely browned, great-tasting crust—just be sure you have the range exhaust hood on high.

1 1/2 pounds Yukon Gold or red-skinned potatoes, scrubbed but unpeeled, cut into 1-inch pieces

1/2 cup plus 3 tablespoons vegetable oil

1 sirloin steak, about 1 1/4 pounds and 1 inch thick

2 tablespoons sherry or cider vinegar

One 10- to 12-ounce package baby spinach

2 ounces Roquefort cheese, crumbled (about 1/2 cup)

1 Preheat oven to 400°F. Toss potatoes and 2 tablespoons oil in a roasting pan. Season with 1/2 teaspoon salt and 1/4 teaspoon pepper. Roast, occasionally scraping up and turning potatoes with a metal spatula, until they are tender and golden brown, about 1 hour.

2 About 15 minutes before potatoes are done, pour 1 tablespoon oil into large, heavy skillet (such as cast iron) over high heat. Tilt skillet to film bottom with oil, and pour out excess oil. Heat skillet over high heat until very hot. Season steak on both sides with 1/2 teaspoon salt and 1/4 teaspoon pepper. Add steak and cook until underside

is browned, about 2 minutes. Turn and brown other side for 2 minutes. Turn again and reduce the heat to medium. Cook for 3 minutes more. Turn the steak and continue cooking until steak feels somewhat firm but also slightly soft when pressed in the center for medium-rare meat, 2 to 3 minutes. Transfer steak to a carving board and let stand 5 minutes.

3   Meanwhile, whisk vinegar, $1/4$ teaspoon salt, and $1/8$ teaspoon pepper in medium bowl. Gradually whisk in remaining $1/2$ cup oil. Add spinach and toss. Spread spinach on a serving platter. Cut steak crosswise into $1/2$-inch-thick slices and arrange steak over spinach. Scatter potatoes around the steak and sprinkle Roquefort over all. Pour carving juices over salad, too. Serve right away.

4 TO 6 SERVINGS

other ideas

SIMPLE TIP *I've made this with shell steak and rib-eye steak, too, and they are great. You can use a tougher cut, such as London broil, flank, or skirt, but these would be better marinated and grilled. Just don't use a marinade that would conflict with the Roquefort cheese.*

VARIATION *Substitute any blue-veined cheese for the Roquefort. If you don't like blue cheese, sprinkle the salad with shredded extra-sharp Cheddar.*

Tortellini, Turkey, and Heirloom Tomato Salad

Here's a salad for a warm late-summer evening, when tomatoes are at their peak and a simple prepared meal is the order of the day. If your delicatessen roasts turkey breast every day for sandwiches, so much the better. For the benefit of full color and flavor, select tomatoes of different hues—red and green zebra are a favorite combination. The recipe purposely uses a pound of tortellini to provide leftovers for the next day's lunch.

$1/2$ pound roasted turkey breast

3 scallions

2 large heirloom-style tomatoes

1 pound frozen cheese-filled tortellini

2 tablespoons red wine vinegar

1 garlic clove, crushed through a press

$1/2$ cup extra-virgin olive oil

PREP *Remove skin from turkey. Cut meat into $3/4$-inch chunks. Slice scallions (white and green parts) into thin rounds. Cut tomatoes into $3/4$-inch dice.*

1. Bring large pot of lightly salted water to a boil over high heat. Add tortellini and cook, stirring occasionally, until tortellini are tender, about 10 minutes. Drain and rinse under cold running water.

2. Whisk vinegar, garlic, $1/4$ teaspoon salt, and $1/4$ teaspoon pepper in medium bowl. Gradually whisk in olive oil.

3. Add tortellini, turkey, tomatoes, and scallions to bowl and mix well. Serve immediately or cover and refrigerate for up to 1 day.

6 SERVINGS

other ideas

SIMPLE TIP *While I usually chop my garlic cloves, there are occasions when it should be crushed through a press. Chopping is fine when the garlic will be softened by cooking. But when the garlic will be served raw and the garlic bits will be rough on the tongue, it is better to crush it into a puree with a garlic press.*

VARIATION *Substitute cheese ravioli for the tortellini.*

Tuna, Sun-Dried Tomato, and White Bean Salad

Salads like this one often grace the antipasti table at Italy's trattorias, where it is served as an appetizing first course. The beans make it substantial enough to be the main dish at a supper or lunch, which is how it is offered here. Try to make it a couple of hours ahead so the flavors have a chance to marry.

1 $^1/_2$ tablespoons freshly squeezed lemon juice

1 garlic clove

$^1/_3$ cup extra-virgin olive oil

Two 15- to 19-ounce cans white kidney (cannellini) beans, drained and rinsed

One 6 $^1/_2$-ounce can tuna in olive oil, drained and flaked

$^1/_3$ cup drained and sliced oil-packed sun-dried tomatoes

$^1/_4$ cup finely chopped red onion

2 tablespoons chopped fresh parsley or basil

1   Whisk lemon juice, garlic, $^1/_4$ teaspoon salt, and $^1/_8$ teaspoon freshly ground pepper in medium bowl. Gradually whisk in olive oil.

2   Add beans, tuna, tomatoes, onion, and parsley. Cover and refrigerate to blend flavors, about 2 hours.

3 Remove from refrigerator about 30 minutes before serving. Serve at room temperature.

4 SERVINGS

other ideas

SIMPLE TIP *Mediterranean cooks have been preserving tuna in olive oil for years. Some domestic brands are now following suit, and you can find them in the canned fish department at the supermarket. Or, look for imported tuna in olive oil at stores with Italian products. You can substitute tuna in vegetable oil or water, if you wish.*

VARIATION *Substitute 4 ounces thinly sliced salami, cut into thin strips, for the tuna.*

the simpler the better Warm and Wonderful Casseroles

Barbecued Kielbasa and Three-Bean Bake

There are times when nothing but a rib-sticking casserole will satisfy, and they don't make them much heartier than this sausage and bean mixture. Serve it with chunks of corn bread.

1 tablespoon vegetable oil

1 pound kielbasa sausage

1 medium onion

One 15- to 19-ounce can navy beans

One 15- to 19-ounce can pinto beans

One 15- to 19-ounce can white kidney (cannellini) beans

1 cup barbecue sauce

$1/2$ cup lager beer, apple juice, or cider

1 Preheat oven to 350°F. Heat oil in large skillet over medium heat. Add sausage and cook, turning once, until sausage is browned on both sides, about 6 minutes. Add onion and cook until softened, about 5 minutes more.

2 Add navy, pinto, and kidney beans, barbecue sauce, and beer. Bring to a simmer.

3 Transfer to 2-quart covered casserole. Cover and bake until slightly thickened, about 30 minutes. Serve hot.

4 TO 6 SERVINGS

other ideas

VARIATIONS *Like it spicy? Use hot links instead of kielbasa.*

Stir in $1/2$ cup coarsely chopped dried apples along with the beer.

Quick Cassoulet

Cassoulet, the glorious bean stew, gets its hearty flavor from a time-consuming mélange of goose confit, pork sausage, and chunks of lamb. When I have made cassoulet according to the book, it took three or four days. Now, I make this faux cassoulet, which may not be as complicated, but is every bit as satisfying. Perhaps the fact that it takes about an hour to make from start to serving instead of four days is part of the satisfaction.

1 ham steak with the round bone, about 1 pound

1 medium onion

2 garlic cloves

Three 15- to 19-ounce cans white kidney (cannellini) beans

1 tablespoon plus 1 teaspoon olive oil

One 14-ounce can chopped tomatoes in juice, drained

1 teaspoon herbes de Provence (see *Simple Tip*), or $1/4$ teaspoon each dried
thyme, rosemary, basil, and oregano

$1/4$ cup plain dry bread crumbs

PREP *Cut ham off bone into bite-size pieces; reserve bone. Chop onion. Finely chop garlic. Drain beans in colander, reserving liquid. Rinse beans.*

1. Preheat oven to 350°F. Heat 1 tablespoon olive oil in a medium nonstick skillet over medium heat. Add ham and cook, stirring occasionally, until it is browned, about 6 minutes. Add onion and garlic and cook, stirring occasionally, until onion softens, about 3 minutes. Add tomatoes and herbs and bring to a simmer.

2. Mix ham mixture, beans, and reserved ham bone in 2- to 2 1/2-quart ovenproof casserole. Add 1 cup reserved bean liquid and mix well (discard remaining bean liquid). Sprinkle with bread crumbs and drizzle with remaining teaspoon olive oil.

3. Bake, occasionally basting bread crumbs with cooking juices (use a large spoon to press down into beans and collect the liquid), until cassoulet is bubbling and crumbs form a thin crust, about 45 minutes. Let stand for 5 minutes, then serve hot. Look out for the ham bone!

6 SERVINGS

other ideas

SIMPLE TIP *Herbes de Provence is no longer a specialty item that can be found only at fancy gourmet shops. Look for it in your supermarket's spice rack. Or, you can approximate the traditional blend by mixing 1 tablespoon each dried thyme, basil, rosemary, and oregano. If you have them, add 2 teaspoons dried savory and 1 teaspoon each dried lavender (buy an edible variety and not the kind used in potpourri) and fennel. Stored in a jar in a cool, dark cabinet, the blend will keep for up to 6 months.*

DRESS IT UP *Use a 3-quart casserole. Brown 6 chicken thighs in a nonstick skillet over medium-high heat, about 6 minutes. Place in the bottom of the casserole, and add the beans.*

VARIATION *Substitute smoked sausage, such as kielbasa or garlic sausage, for the ham.*

Corn and Ham Pudding

This melt-in-your-mouth treat has comfort food written all over it. If you wish, make it with fresh corn kernels cut off the cob.

1 small onion

1 small red bell pepper

2 tablespoons butter

$1/2$ pound smoked ham, cut into bite-size cubes

2 cups thawed frozen corn kernels

$1 1/4$ cups half-and-half or milk

3 large eggs

$1/2$ cup (2 ounces) shredded sharp Cheddar cheese

PREP *Chop onion into $1/2$-inch dice. Remove and discard seeds and ribs from red pepper; cut into $1/2$-inch dice.*

1   Position rack in center of oven and preheat oven to 325°F. Melt butter over medium-high heat in medium skillet. Add ham and cook until lightly browned, about 5 minutes. Add onion and red pepper and cook until softened, about 5 minutes more. Spread in $11 1/2$ x 8-inch baking dish.

2   Meanwhile, puree 1 cup corn with half-and-half, eggs, $1/4$ teaspoon salt, and $1/4$ teaspoon freshly ground black pepper in blender. Pour into medium bowl and stir in remaining 1 cup corn. Pour over ham mixture in dish and sprinkle with Cheddar cheese.

3   Bake until knife inserted 1 inch from center of custard comes out clean, about 45 minutes. Let stand for 5 minutes. Serve hot.

4 SERVINGS

other ideas

VARIATION *Substitute turkey or pork Italian sausage, casings removed, for the ham. Cook until sausage is completely cooked through, about 8 minutes, before adding onion and red pepper.*

Chicken and Bean Casserole, Burrito Style

This casserole is as homey as they come, with a simple, unassuming demeanor. It's no beauty, but it is a real crowd pleaser and lots of fun to eat. Spread spoonfuls of the casserole onto a warm tortilla, roll it up, and go for it.

1 medium onion

2 garlic cloves

1 $1/4$ pounds ground chicken

One $14 1/2$-ounce can chopped tomatoes with jalapeños

Two 16-ounce cans refried beans

$1/2$ cup (2 ounces) shredded sharp Cheddar cheese

Warm flour tortillas, for serving

Tomato salsa, for serving

PREP *Chop onion. Finely chop garlic.*

1 Preheat oven to 350°F. Cook chicken, onion, and garlic in large nonstick skillet, stirring and breaking up chicken with a spoon, until chicken is cooked through, about 8 minutes. Pour off fat in skillet. Add tomatoes and jalapeños with juices and bring to a simmer. Cook until tomato juices thicken, about 5 minutes. Season with salt and freshly ground pepper to taste.

2 Transfer chicken mixture to 2-quart casserole. Spread beans over chicken. Sprinkle with cheese. Bake until juices are bubbling, about 25 minutes.

3 To serve, spread a heaping spoonful of bean casserole onto each warm tortilla. Add salsa, roll up tortilla, and eat.

4 SERVINGS

other ideas

SIMPLE TIP *Look on the label of the refried beans to know what you're getting. Many brands contain lard, which does provide the most authentic Mexican flavor, but that may not be your preference. If you wish, use vegetarian or fat-free refried beans, which will be lard-free.*

DRESS IT UP *Serve the casserole with shredded iceberg lettuce, sour cream, guacamole, and additional Cheddar cheese all for tucking into the burritos.*

VARIATION *For a spicier version, after the chicken is cooked and the fat has been poured off, stir 1 tablespoon chili powder into the skillet.*

Farmhouse Chicken Pot Pie

Is chicken pot pie the ultimate one-dish meal? If you have a round of homemade pie dough in the freezer, you can whip up a satisfyingly retro pot pie in no time at all. This streamlined version also uses frozen vegetables, which are used to great advantage here. Old-fashioned? Yes. But, it is also irresistible.

3 tablespoons butter

1 pound boneless and skinless chicken thighs, cut into 1-inch pieces

$1/2$ cup finely chopped onion

One 10-ounce package defrosted frozen mixed vegetables

$1/4$ cup all-purpose flour

2 cups milk, heated

1 round Homemade Pie Dough (page 66) or store-bought refrigerated pie dough

1   Preheat oven to 375°F. Melt butter in medium skillet over medium heat. Add chicken and cook, stirring occasionally, until chicken is lightly browned, about 8 minutes. Add onion and cook until soft, about 3 minutes. Add vegetables and cook for 2 minutes (this helps evaporate any surface moisture from the vegetables). Sprinkle with flour and mix well. Stir in milk and bring to a simmer. Reduce heat to medium-low and simmer, stirring often, for 2 minutes. Season with salt and freshly ground pepper to taste.

2 Pour chicken filling into 9 1/2-inch deep-dish pie pan. Use your fingertip to moisten edge of pan with water. Fit pie dough round over pan and press dough onto edge of pan. Cut a few slits in top of pie dough.

3 Place pie on baking sheet. Bake until crust is golden brown and filling is bubbling through vents, 35 to 45 minutes. Cool for a few minutes, then serve hot.

6 SERVINGS

other ideas

SIMPLE TIP *Heat the milk for the filling in a microwave on high or in a small saucepan until small bubbles appear around the edges of the milk. The hot milk will make the sauce come to a boil much more quickly than cold milk.*

DRESS IT UP *To glaze the crust, mix 1 large egg yolk and 1 teaspoon milk until well combined. Brush some of the egg yolk in a thin layer over the crust before baking.*

Stir 1 tablespoon chopped fresh parsley or tarragon (or a combination) into the filling.

VARIATION *For turkey pot pie, substitute turkey tenderloins or turkey London broil (which are thick cuts) cut into 1-inch pieces for the chicken breast. Do not use thinly sliced turkey breast cutlets, which could dry out and toughen in this dish.*

Homemade Pie Dough

To top a casserole with pie dough, one could simply go out and buy refrigerated pie dough—they'll do in a pinch. But, if you are a from-scratch cook like me, here's a recipe.

> 1 $1/4$ cups unbleached all-purpose flour
>
> 7 tablespoons ($1/2$ stick plus 3 tablespoons) butter, chilled, cut into $1/2$-inch pieces
>
> 3 tablespoons ice water, as needed

1   To make dough in a food processor, fit work bowl with metal blade. Add flour and $1/8$ teaspoon salt and pulse a few times to combine them. Add butter and pulse about 10 times, until mixture looks like coarse bread crumbs with a few pea-size pieces of butter. Sprinkle ice water over the flour mixture, and pulse *just until* dough looks moistened. Do not process into a ball—if dough comes together when you pinch some between your thumb and forefinger, it is moist enough. If too dry, add 2 teaspoons additional water and pulse a few times. Gather up the dough and press into a thick disk.

To make by hand, mix flour and $1/8$ teaspoon salt in a medium bowl. Using a pastry blender, cut butter into flour until the mixture looks like coarse bread crumbs with a few pea-size pieces of butter. Stirring with a fork, gradually stir in enough water until dough is evenly moistened and is beginning to clump together. Gather up dough and press into a thick disk.

In either case, refrigerate dough for at least 30 minutes or up to 1 day. If the dough is well chilled and hard, let it stand at room temperature for about 20 minutes to soften slightly without losing its chill.

2   Lightly flour a work surface. Unwrap dough and sprinkle top with flour. Roll out dough into a 10- to 11-inch round about $1/8$ inch thick. The dough can be used immediately or frozen for future use.

MAKES 1 PIE CRUST FOR A 9-INCH PIE

Stuffed Chicken Breast and Rice Casserole

One of my rules for easy cooking is to use ingredients that deliver lots of flavor. For example, take a supermarket cheese like Boursin. Instead of having to deal with a variety of herbs, plus cream cheese, garlic, and pepper, Boursin provides these flavors in one fell swoop. Here I use Boursin to stuff chicken breasts that are nestled into mushroom-flavored rice and baked for an elegant casserole.

10 ounces cremini (baby portobello) mushrooms

4 boneless and skinless chicken breasts, about 8 ounces each

One 5$\frac{1}{5}$-ounce package creamy herbed cheese, such as Boursin

2 tablespoons plain dry bread crumbs

3 tablespoons butter

$\frac{1}{3}$ cup chopped shallots

1 cup long-grain rice

2 tablespoons chopped fresh parsley

PREP *Thinly slice mushrooms.*

1 Preheat oven to 350°F. Lightly butter an 11$\frac{1}{2}$ x 8-inch baking dish. Pound chicken breasts between sheets of plastic wrap until about $\frac{1}{4}$ inch thick. Season with $\frac{1}{2}$ teaspoon salt and $\frac{1}{4}$ teaspoon freshly ground pepper. Mix cheese and bread crumbs

in small bowl. Shape into four 2-inch-long logs. Place 1 log in center of 1 breast, roll up, and secure closed with wooden toothpicks. Repeat with remaining chicken and cheese.

2   Melt 1 tablespoon of butter in large skillet over medium-high heat. Add chicken and brown on all sides, about 5 minutes. Transfer to plate. Add remaining 2 tablespoons butter to skillet. Add mushrooms and cook until tender, about 6 minutes. Add shallots and cook until wilted, about 2 minutes. Stir in rice, 1$^3/_4$ cups water, and $^1/_2$ teaspoon salt. Bring to a boil.

3   Transfer rice mixture to baking dish. Arrange chicken breasts on top and cover with aluminum foil. Bake until rice has absorbed liquid and is tender, 30 to 35 minutes. Sprinkle with parsley and serve hot. (Remind guests to remove toothpicks from chicken.)

4 SERVINGS

other ideas

SIMPLE TIP *Buy large, plump chicken breasts. If much smaller than 8 ounces each, they will be difficult to pound to a large enough size for holding the cheese.*

DRESS IT UP *Substitute $^1/_2$ cup chicken broth and $^1/_4$ cup dry white wine for the water.*

Spiced Lamb with Dried Cherries in Acorn Squash

Inspired by the flavors of the Middle East, this meal comes in its own edible container. Acorn squash takes time to cook through. If you need to speed things up, use the microwave variation.

2 acorn squash, 1^1/$_2$ pounds each

^{1}/$_3$ cup dried sour cherries

1 medium onion

1 large egg

2 tablespoons tomato paste

1^1/$_2$ pounds ground lamb

^{1}/$_4$ cup plain dry bread crumbs

1^1/$_2$ teaspoons curry powder

PREP *Cut each squash in half lengthwise; scoop out and discard seeds. Soak cherries in ^{1}/$_2$ cup warm water to plump; drain. Grate onion on box grater.*

1 Preheat oven to 350°F. Line baking sheet with aluminum foil; oil foil. Place squash, cut side down, on baking sheet and bake until beginning to soften, about 45 minutes.

2 Beat egg and tomato paste in medium bowl to dissolve paste. Add lamb, drained cherries, grated onion, bread crumbs, curry powder, and 1 teaspoon salt and mix well.

3 Turn squash cut sides up. Fill squash with equal amounts of lamb mixture. Bake until lamb filling is browned and shows no sign of pink in the center when cut with tip of sharp knife, about 45 minutes. Let stand 5 minutes. Serve hot.

4 SERVINGS

other ideas

SIMPLE TIP *Ground lamb can be found at Middle Eastern grocers and many super-markets. If you have the opportunity to speak to the butcher, ask for lean ground lamb, as lamb can be fatty. Ground sirloin or ground round can be substituted for the lamb.*

VARIATION *Do not cut squash in half. In Step 1, pierce each squash a few times with a fork. Place the squash in a microwave oven and cook on high until the squash begins to soften, about 6 minutes. Let stand 5 minutes, then cut each squash in half, discarding the seeds. Stuff the squash with the lamb mixture and bake as directed in a conventional oven.*

Enchilada Pie with Sausage and Eggs

This mildly spiced supper dish can also be served for brunch. Try to find fresh chorizo, which is spicier than Italian sausage. If using the latter, add 1 tablespoon chili powder to the sausage after cooking the onion. Now, how to choose between red chile or green tomatillo chile enchilada sauce?

1 medium onion

7 corn tortillas (6-inch diameter)

1 tablespoon olive oil

$3/4$ pound fresh chorizo or Italian hot sausage, casings removed

4 large eggs, beaten

One 10-ounce can red or green enchilada sauce, heated

1 cup (4 ounces) shredded Monterey jack or mozzarella cheese

1   Place tortillas directly on oven racks and preheat oven to 350°F. Remove tortillas after 10 minutes—they will dry and feel leathery as they cool. Cut 1 tortilla in half. Lightly oil 9-inch pie pan.

2   Heat olive oil in large nonstick skillet over medium heat. Add sausage and cook, occasionally stirring and breaking up sausage with a side of a spoon, until sausage loses its pink color, about 8 minutes. Add onion and cook until onion softens, about

5 minutes. Pour off fat in skillet. Add eggs, $1/4$ teaspoon salt, and $1/4$ teaspoon pepper and cook, stirring often, until eggs are scrambled and barely set, about 2 minutes.

3   Arrange $3^1/2$ tortillas to cover bottom of pie pan. Pour half of sauce over tortillas. Top with sausage-egg mixture, cover with remaining $3^1/2$ tortillas. Spread remaining sauce over tortillas and sprinkle with cheese. Bake until sauce bubbles around edges and cheese melts, about 20 minutes. Let stand 5 minutes. Cut into wedges to serve.

4 SERVINGS

other ideas

SIMPLE TIP *Don't confuse soft, fresh chorizo with the hard, smoked version. Fresh chorizo looks very much like regular pork sausage, although it is colored red with ground chiles. You'll find fresh chorizo at most Latino supermarkets.*

DRESS IT UP *Sprinkle the top of the pie with chopped fresh cilantro and serve with a dollop of sour cream.*

VARIATION *Add 1 jalapeño, seeded and minced, and 2 finely chopped garlic cloves to the sausage along with the onion.*

Baker's Lamb Chops with Potatoes and Green Beans

the simpler the better

Back when not every home had a stove, French villagers would bring their roasts to the town baker and use *his* oven. A popular recipe was lamb roasted over potatoes, an idea, simplified here with lamb chops and bolstered with green beans, that lends itself to the one-pot concept.

2 pounds baking potatoes, such as Burbank or russet

1 large onion

2 garlic cloves

12 ounces green beans

3 tablespoons olive oil

4 shoulder lamb chops, 8 ounces each

1 tablespoon chopped fresh rosemary, or 1 teaspoon crumbled dried

PREP *Peel potatoes and cut into $1/8$-inch-thick rounds. Chop onion. Finely chop garlic. Trim green beans and cut into 1-inch lengths.*

1 Preheat oven to 350°F. Heat 1 tablespoon olive oil in a large, ovenproof skillet (preferably nonstick) over medium-high heat. Season lamb chops with $1/2$ teaspoon salt and $1/4$ teaspoon freshly ground pepper. In batches, if necessary, add to skillet and cook, turning once, until browned on all sides, about 5 minutes. Transfer to bowl. Pour out

fat in skillet. Return skillet to medium-high heat, add 1 cup water, and bring to boil, scraping up browned bits in pan. Pour over lamb chops.

2 Wipe out skillet. Reduce heat to medium. Heat remaining 2 tablespoons olive oil in skillet. Add potatoes and cook, turning occasionally, until they begin to lose raw look, about 10 minutes. Sprinkle with onion, garlic, and rosemary and cook until onion softens, about 5 minutes more. Season with $1/4$ teaspoon salt and $1/4$ teaspoon freshly ground pepper.

3 Pour juices from bowl evenly over potatoes, then top with lamb chops. Cover and bake 10 minutes. Scatter green beans over potatoes, cover, and continue baking until lamb is tender, about 5 minutes more. Uncover and let stand for 5 minutes before serving.

4 SERVINGS

other ideas

SIMPLE TIP *A plastic V-shaped slicer makes quick work of slicing potatoes and other vegetable prep chores. It is a reasonably priced, and much easier to use, version of the mandoline, a stainless-steel slicing tool that can be daunting in price and execution. You can find these slicers at kitchenware stores.*

DRESS IT UP *Sprinkle the potatoes with $1/2$ cup freshly grated Parmesan cheese before adding the lamb chops.*

Substitute chicken broth for the water in Step 1.

Moussaka with Roasted Eggplant

In most Greek *tavernas*, the cook wouldn't dream of making moussaka without frying the eggplant in loads of olive oil. This version roasts the eggplant instead, something that can be easily accomplished while preparing the other components. Topped with yogurt custard, this is moussaka for the gods, even though it is much easier than the classic method.

2 medium eggplants, about 1 $\frac{1}{4}$ pounds each

5 tablespoons olive oil

1 $\frac{1}{4}$ pounds ground lamb

One 16-ounce jar marinara sauce

$\frac{1}{4}$ teaspoon ground cinnamon

4 large eggs

2 cups plain yogurt, preferably Greek whole-milk yogurt (see *Simple Tip*)

PREP *Trim eggplants and slice each crosswise into 12 to 14 slices $\frac{1}{2}$ inch thick.*

1   Position oven racks in top third and center of oven and preheat oven to 450°F. Line 2 large baking sheets with aluminum foil and oil well. Arrange eggplant slices (they can overlap slightly) on baking sheets and brush with 4 tablespoons olive oil. Bake until tender, about 20 minutes.

2   Meanwhile, heat remaining tablespoon olive oil in large skillet over medium heat. Add lamb and cook, stirring and breaking up meat with a spoon, until beginning to brown, about 10 minutes. Pour off fat in skillet. Add marinara sauce and cinnamon and bring to a simmer. Season with salt and freshly ground pepper to taste.

3   Beat eggs in medium bowl, then stir in yogurt to combine. Add $1/2$ teaspoon salt and $1/4$ teaspoon freshly ground pepper. Place half of eggplant slices, overlapping as needed, in baking dish. Top with lamb sauce, remaining eggplant, and yogurt custard. Bake until custard looks set when pan is gently shaken, about 25 minutes. Let stand 5 minutes and serve hot.

6 SERVINGS

other ideas

SIMPLE TIPS *You'll find Greek yogurt, which has a thicker consistency than most American brands, at Mediterranean delicatessens and many supermarkets. It comes in non-fat, low-fat, and whole-milk versions. Every major market has its own local brand—Total is well distributed on the East Coast. If you can't find it, use a domestic yogurt, but stick to the whole-milk or low-fat versions, as nonfat may not hold up in the oven as a topping.*

Domestic yogurt should be drained before using in this recipe. Line a wire sieve with mois-tened paper towels and place it over a bowl. Place $2 1/2$ cups yogurt in the sieve, then place a saucer on the yogurt. Refrigerate and let drain until $1/2$ cup whey collects in the bowl, about 2 hours. Discard the whey.

VARIATION *Use ground round instead of the ground lamb.*

White and Green Pizza

Making pizza at home is a snap now that many supermarkets carry pizza dough in the refrigerated or frozen section (I know people who buy dough from a friendly pizzeria), and it is very satisfying to serve piping-hot pizza straight from your own oven. Because this pizza doesn't have tomato sauce, it stays nice and crispy. You'll need a pizza pan or baking sheet for baking the dough.

$1/2$ pound mozzarella cheese, preferably fresh, but processed is fine

Two 10-ounce boxes thawed frozen chopped spinach

1 pound pizza dough, thawed if frozen

$2/3$ cup freshly grated Parmesan cheese (about 3 ounces)

Olive oil, for brushing

3 tablespoons chopped fresh basil

$1/2$ teaspoon crushed red pepper flakes

PREP *Shred mozzarella. A handful at a time, squeeze as much moisture as possible from chopped spinach.*

1   Position rack in bottom third of oven and preheat oven to 450°F. Stretch pizza dough into 12-inch round on pizza pan or large baking sheet.

2   Leaving 1-inch border, sprinkle dough with $1/3$ cup Parmesan. Scatter clumps of

spinach over dough. Sprinkle with mozzarella, then remaining $1/3$ cup Parmesan. Brush exposed dough with olive oil.

3 Bake until crust is golden brown, about 17 minutes. Sprinkle with basil and red pepper flakes. Cut into wedges and serve hot.

MAKES ONE 12-INCH PIZZA, 3 TO 4 SERVINGS

other ideas

SIMPLE TIP *Because homemade pizza is a special treat (although you may find it so easy that it becomes a staple), I use fresh mozzarella. You'll find it at cheese stores, natural food store chains, and many supermarkets, usually stored in brine.*

DRESS IT UP *Just before serving, drizzle the pizza with garlic-flavored olive oil.*

VARIATIONS *Use smoked mozzarella instead of plain mozzarella.*

For white and red pizza, substitute 1 cup coarsely chopped sun-dried tomatoes for the spinach.

Pork Chops with Cheddar-Garlic Grits

Grits—coarsely cracked dried hominy—are a Southern favorite, but more Yankees could stand to get to know them. They are bland, all the better to show off flavors like sharp Cheddar cheese and zesty garlic. Tuck in some browned chops and bake it all in a warming casserole.

2 tablespoons olive oil

4 center-cut pork chops, about 8 ounces each

$1/2$ cup chopped red bell pepper

1 cup fresh or thawed frozen corn kernels

2 garlic cloves

$3/4$ cup quick-cooking hominy grits

$1/2$ cup (2 ounces) shredded sharp Cheddar cheese

2 tablespoons chopped fresh parsley

1 Preheat oven to 350°F. Heat 1 tablespoon olive oil in large ovenproof skillet with a lid over medium-high heat. Season chops with $1/2$ teaspoon salt and $1/4$ teaspoon freshly ground pepper. Place in skillet and cook, turning once, until browned on both sides, about 6 minutes. Transfer to a plate.

2 Add remaining tablespoon olive oil to skillet. Add red pepper and cook, stirring often, until softened, about 3 minutes. Add corn and garlic, and cook until garlic is

fragrant, about 1 minute. Add 3 cups water and $1/4$ teaspoon salt and bring to boil. Stir in grits and return to boil. Return chops to skillet and cover tightly.

3   Bake for 25 minutes. Remove lid and stir grits (they will look soupy) around chops as best as you can. Sprinkle with cheese. Return to oven and bake, uncovered, until cheese melts and grits thicken, about 5 minutes. Sprinkle with parsley and serve hot.

4 SERVINGS

other ideas

SIMPLE TIP *For this recipe, when buying grits, be sure to get the quick-cooking variety and not instant (which would cook too quickly) or traditional (which would cook too slowly).*

VARIATION *Add 1 medium onion, chopped, to the skillet along with the red pepper.*

Zucchini and Herbed Cheese Quiche

Here's another recipe that uses herbed cream cheese to provide lots of flavor with little effort. Quiche has become popular again. Combined with sautéed zucchini, this could become one of your favorites, too.

1 large zucchini, well scrubbed

One 11-inch round Homemade Pie Dough (page 66), or use store-bought refrigerated pie dough

1 tablespoon butter

3 large eggs

1 1/2 cups half-and-half

One 5 1/5-ounce package herbed cream cheese, such as Boursin

PREP *Cut zucchini lengthwise, then into 1/4-inch-thick half-moons.*

1 Place baking sheet in oven and preheat oven to 425°F. Line 9-inch pie dish with pie dough, fluting edges of dough. Refrigerate until needed.

2 Heat butter in large skillet over medium-high heat. Add zucchini and cook, stirring occasionally, until zucchini is tender and lightly browned, 10 to 12 minutes. Whisk eggs, half-and-half, 1/4 teaspoon salt, and 1/4 teaspoon freshly ground pepper in medium bowl. Crumble cheese in pie shell. Top with zucchini, then pour in custard.

3   Place on hot baking sheet in oven. Bake 15 minutes. Reduce oven temperature to 350°F. Continue baking until knife inserted 1 inch from center of custard comes out clean, about 30 minutes more. Cool 10 minutes. Serve warm or cooled to room temperature.

6 TO 8 SERVINGS

other ideas

SIMPLE TIP *Baking the quiche in the bottom third of the oven on a hot baking sheet helps to create a crisp, browned bottom crust that discourages sogginess. Pyrex pie dishes are excellent because they allow you to check the progression of the bottom crust's browning.*

VARIATION *Add $1/2$ cup chopped red bell pepper to zucchini.*

Ravioli "Lasagna"

The idea behind this baked dish is to provide the heartiness of lasagna without the tedium of boiling and layering noodles and making all sorts of fillings. Cheese-stuffed ravioli contributes the ricotta and the pasta, and the rest of the classic ingredients are found in the meaty tomato sauce. There's no need to simmer the sauce any longer than recommended—after all, it will cook for an additional 30 minutes in the oven.

1 medium onion
2 garlic cloves
1 pound cheese-filled ravioli
1 tablespoon olive oil
$1\frac{1}{4}$ pounds lean ground beef
One 28-ounce can crushed tomatoes in puree
$1\frac{1}{2}$ teaspoons Italian seasoning
1 cup (4 ounces) shredded mozzarella cheese

PREP *Chop onion. Finely chop garlic.*

1 Preheat oven to 350°F. Lightly oil 9 x 13-inch baking dish. Bring a large pot of lightly salted water to a boil over high heat. Add ravioli and cook until barely tender, about 10 minutes. Do not overcook; they will cook more in the oven.

2   Meanwhile, heat olive oil in medium saucepan over medium heat. Add onion and cook, stirring occasionally, until translucent, about 5 minutes. Add garlic and stir until fragrant, about 1 minute. Add ground beef and cook, breaking up the meat with a spoon, until it loses its raw look, about 7 minutes. Add tomatoes and Italian seasoning, and bring to a boil. Reduce heat to medium-low and simmer for 10 minutes. Season with salt and pepper to taste.

3   Drain ravioli well. Spread $1/2$ cup sauce in baking dish. Layer with half of ravioli, half of sauce. Top with remaining ravioli and sauce. Sprinkle mozzarella over top. Bake until sauce is bubbling and cheese is melted, about 30 minutes.

4 TO 6 SERVINGS

other ideas

SIMPLE TIP *When shopping for canned crushed tomatoes, avoid those that say "from concentrate," as their flavor and texture are lacking. When you find a brand that you like, save the label so you know what to look for the next time you go to the market.*

DRESS IT UP *For a hint of smokiness, substitute smoked mozzarella for the regular mozzarella.*

VARIATION *There are a few substitution options for the ground beef. Try this with Italian sausages (either pork or turkey) and reduce the Italian seasoning to 1 teaspoon. Or use ground turkey.*

Baked Shrimp with Scallions, Tomatoes, and Feta

When dinner needs to be on the table fast, you can rely on this colorful and flavorful dish. You have the option of spooning the shrimp onto a bed of rice or orzo, or just using crusty bread to soak up the juice.

4 scallions

2 garlic cloves

$1\frac{1}{2}$ pounds large (21–25 count) shrimp

2 tablespoons extra-virgin olive oil

One 28-ounce can chopped tomatoes in juice

$\frac{1}{2}$ cup crumbled feta cheese

2 tablespoons chopped fresh dill or oregano

PREP *Chop white and green parts of scallions. Finely chop garlic. Peel and devein shrimp.*

1 Preheat oven to 400°F. Heat olive oil in a large ovenproof skillet over medium heat. Add scallions and garlic and cook, stirring often, until scallions wilt, about 2 minutes. Add tomatoes and their juice and bring to a boil. Cook until tomato juices thicken, about 5 minutes. Season with freshly ground pepper to taste.

2 Remove from heat and stir in shrimp. Sprinkle with feta cheese.

3 Bake until cheese melts and shrimp are firm and opaque, about 10 minutes. Sprinkle with dill and serve hot.

4 SERVINGS

other ideas

SIMPLE TIP *My favorite brands of tomatoes are organic and use naturally derived citric acid in the processing. Get the convenient chopped tomatoes in juice, which come in many different versions—fire-roasted or plain, with jalapeños, with basil and garlic, or with Italian seasonings.*

Turkey Chili with Polenta Topping

Tamale pie has been the friend of many busy cooks for generations. With the advent of precooked polenta, which is cornmeal, after all, it has become even quicker. And with lean ground turkey, even more healthful.

1 medium onion

2 garlic cloves

1$\frac{1}{4}$ pounds ground turkey

1 tablespoon chili powder

One 14$\frac{1}{2}$-ounce can chopped tomatoes with chiles

One 15- to 19-ounce can black beans, drained and rinsed

One 18-ounce roll precooked polenta, cut into 18 rounds

1 cup shredded sharp Cheddar cheese, about 4 ounces

PREP *Chop onion. Finely chop garlic.*

1 Preheat oven to 350°F. Lightly oil 13 x 9-inch baking dish. Cook turkey, onion, and garlic in large nonstick skillet over medium-high heat, stirring often to break up turkey with a spoon, until turkey loses its raw look, about 10 minutes.

2 Tilt skillet to pour off liquid. Return to heat, stir in chili powder, and stir for 30 seconds. Add tomatoes and chiles with juices and black beans. Simmer to blend flavors,

about 10 minutes. Season with salt and freshly ground pepper to taste. Spread turkey chili in baking dish. Top with overlapping rounds of polenta. Sprinkle with cheese.

3   Bake until chili is bubbling and cheese melts, about 20 minutes. Serve hot.

4 TO 6 SERVINGS

other ideas

SIMPLE TIP *Precooked polenta is packaged in squat rolls and can usually be found in the refrigerated section of the market (although some aseptically packaged brands can be found in the grocery aisles, sometimes in the pasta section). It is often flavored with sun-dried tomatoes, herbs and garlic, and other seasonings. If you can't find plain polenta, just use the sun-dried tomato version, or another flavor that will complement the chili.*

VARIATION *To make a lower-fat version of this dish, use extra-lean (1% fat) ground turkey breast and reduced-fat cheddar cheese.*

Wild Rice, Chicken Sausage, and Artichoke Heart Casserole

I love nutty-earthy wild rice, which only too often is demoted to side-dish status. In this dish, it is the star of the show. When it comes to exact cooking times, wild rice is notoriously unreliable, so be flexible. If the rice isn't cooked and the liquid has been absorbed, add a bit of hot water to the casserole and continue baking.

One 13-ounce can chicken sausages with mushrooms

1 medium onion

One 10-ounce box frozen artichoke hearts

2 tablespoons olive oil

One 14$\frac{1}{2}$-ounce can chopped tomatoes in juice, drained

1 teaspoon Italian seasoning, or $\frac{1}{2}$ teaspoon each dried basil and oregano

1 cup wild rice, rinsed in a sieve

One 14$\frac{1}{2}$-ounce can chicken broth

PREP *Cut sausages into $\frac{1}{2}$-inch-thick rounds. Chop onion. Defrost artichokes (place in a sieve and run under warm water).*

1 Preheat oven to 325°F. Heat 1 tablespoon olive oil in large ovenproof skillet over medium-high heat. Add sausages and cook, turning occasionally, until lightly browned, about 5 minutes. Transfer sausages to plate.

2   Heat remaining tablespoon olive oil in skillet over medium heat. Add onion and cook, stirring often, until translucent, about 5 minutes. Add reserved sausages, tomatoes, artichokes, and Italian seasoning and bring to a boil. Stir in wild rice, broth, $1/3$ cup water, $1/2$ teaspoon salt, and $1/4$ teaspoon freshly ground pepper and return to boil.

3   Cover tightly and bake until rice is tender and liquid is absorbed, about 1 hour. Remove from oven and let stand for 5 minutes before serving. (If rice is too moist, use a perforated spoon to serve.)

4 TO 6 SERVINGS

other ideas

SIMPLE TIP *Hand-harvested wild rice (typically from the Midwest or Canada) usually takes a bit more time to cook than machine-harvested rice (often grown in California). Some people like wild rice best if it is cooked until it splits and curls, and others prefer it more al dente. The choice is yours.*

DRESS IT UP *I never throw away the rind from Italian Parmesan cheese. When I make this dish, I tuck a 2- to 3-ounce rind into the rice before baking. You may wish to follow suit.*

Pesto Vegetable Shepherd's Pie

Mashed potato–topped shepherd's pie is usually made from ground meat, but it's the topping that gets my attention. Who doesn't love mashed potatoes, especially when slathered over pesto-coated sautéed vegetables?

2 pounds baking potatoes, such as Burbank or russet

4 medium zucchini, well scrubbed

1 red bell pepper

$1/2$ cup sour cream, at room temperature

3 tablespoons butter

2 cups fresh or thawed frozen corn kernels

3 tablespoons store-bought pesto

1 cup (4 ounces) freshly grated Parmesan cheese

PREP *Peel potatoes and cut into 1-inch chunks. Cut zucchini in half lengthwise, then into half-moons. Cut out and discard seeds and ribs from red pepper; cut into $1/2$-inch dice.*

1　Preheat oven to 350°F. Lightly butter 13 x 9-inch baking dish. Place potatoes in large saucepan and add enough lightly salted water to cover. Bring to a boil over high heat. Reduce heat to medium and simmer until tender, about 20 minutes. Drain and return to pot. Add sour cream and mash with potato masher or handheld electric mixer. Season with salt and freshly ground pepper to taste.

2 Meanwhile, heat 2 tablespoons butter in very large skillet over medium-high heat. Add zucchini and red pepper and cook, stirring occasionally, until vegetables are tender, about 12 minutes. Stir in corn and pesto. Season with salt and pepper. Spread vegetables in baking dish. Spread with mashed potatoes and sprinkle with cheese. Cut remaining 1 tablespoon butter into small cubes and sprinkle over potatoes.

3 Bake until topping is tinged with brown and cheese melts, about 20 minutes. Serve hot.

4 TO 6 SERVINGS

other ideas

VARIATION *Add 2 finely chopped garlic cloves to the skillet with the zucchini and red pepper.*

the simpler the better

From the Skillet: Stir-Fries and More

Ginger Beef and Asparagus Stir-Fry

Asian stir-fries are easy to pull off, as long as you have prepared all of the ingredients before you get cooking. And with a minimum of ingredients to chop and slice, as with this ginger-scented dish of beef and asparagus, you will have dinner on the table in much less time than it takes to have Chinese food delivered.

1 large red bell pepper

$1/2$ pound asparagus

2 tablespoons vegetable oil

2 tablespoons shredded fresh ginger (use the large holes of a box grater)

1 pound "stir-fry-cut" boneless top round beef

3 tablespoons soy sauce

2 teaspoons cornstarch

Hot cooked rice, for serving

PREP *Trim and discard seeds and ribs from bell pepper; cut into 2-inch strips about $1/4$ inch wide. Snap off and discard woody stems from asparagus; cut spears on diagonal into 1-inch lengths.*

1 Heat very large empty skillet over high heat until skillet is very hot, about 2 minutes. Add 1 tablespoon oil and swirl to coat bottom of skillet. Add ginger and stir-fry until softened, about 15 seconds. Add red pepper and asparagus and $1/4$ cup water. Cover

and cook until vegetables are crisp-tender, about 2 minutes. Transfer vegetables to platter.

2 Heat remaining tablespoon oil in skillet until very hot. Add beef and stir-fry until beef loses raw look, about 3 minutes. Return vegetables to skillet.

3 Mix 1 cup water and soy sauce in small bowl, sprinkle cornstarch on top, and whisk to dissolve cornstarch. Pour into skillet, mix well, and bring to boil. Season with salt and pepper to taste. Serve hot, spooned over rice.

4 SERVINGS

other ideas

SIMPLE TIP *You don't really need a wok for stir-frying. A very large skillet, about 12 inches in diameter to hold all of the ingredients without crowding, works very well. The secret to successful stir-frying is to thoroughly heat the skillet over high heat before adding the oil and food, a step that helps the ingredients cook evenly and quickly.*

VARIATION *Boneless and skinless chicken breast, cut into thin strips about 2 inches long and 1/4 inch wide, can stand in for the beef. Stir-fry the chicken until cooked through, about 5 minutes, before returning the vegetables to the skillet.*

Spanish Burgers with Chile, Manchego, and Sherry Vinaigrette

These open-faced burgers take advantage of three Spanish foods that are showing up in markets: piquillo red chile, manchego cheese, and sherry vinegar. While these ingredients have distinctions that will produce extraordinary burgers, roasted bell peppers, red wine vinegar, and a sharp cheese like Cheddar will also create a darned good burger.

1 1/2 pounds ground sirloin

6 tablespoons extra-virgin olive oil

3 ounces manchego cheese, thinly sliced

2 tablespoons sherry vinegar

1 garlic clove, crushed through a press

4 slices rustic-style bread, toasted

4 ounces mixed field greens (mesclun)

4 piquillo chiles, drained

1 Mix sirloin, 1 teaspoon salt, and 1/4 teaspoon pepper in medium bowl. Shape into 4 burgers, each about 4 inches in diameter. Heat 1 tablespoon olive oil in a large heavy skillet (preferably cast iron) over medium-high heat.

2 Place burgers in skillet and cook, turning once, until browned on both sides, about 6 minutes for medium-rare burgers. During last minute, top burgers with cheese and cover to melt cheese.

3 Meanwhile, whisk sherry vinegar, garlic, $1/8$ teaspoon salt, and a few grinds of freshly ground pepper in small bowl. Whisk in remaining 5 tablespoons olive oil. For each serving, place 1 slice toasted bread on plate. Top with a handful of greens and a burger. Top burger with chile. Spoon scant 2 tablespoons vinaigrette over burgers and greens, and serve.

4 SERVINGS

other ideas

SIMPLE TIP *Piquillo chiles are small, triangular-shaped red peppers that are slow-roasted for an intense, slightly piquant flavor. Semi firm, tangy manchego cheese is made from sheep's milk and melts beautifully. Sherry vinegar is mellow with a sweet edge. My local natural food market carries all three.*

VARIATIONS *Use another type of roasted red pepper (imported Greek red peppers are also favorites of mine) instead of the piquillo chiles.*

Substitute $1 1/2$ tablespoons red wine vinegar for the sherry vinegar. Red wine vinegar is sharper than sherry vinegar, so you use less.

Sharp Cheddar cheese is a good substitute for the manchego.

Chicken, Basil, and Peanut Stir-Fry

Thai cooking has bright flavors, but you don't really need to get authentic ingredients to create a spicy stir-fry in that cooking's tradition. Of course, if you have access to Thai fish sauce, holy basil, and chiles, you can use them. Otherwise, use supermarket groceries, just as I often do, and you will be perfectly happy with the results.

1 pound boneless and skinless chicken breasts

1 large red bell pepper

1 large shallot

1 jalapeño

2 tablespoons vegetable oil

2 packed cups fresh basil leaves

2 tablespoons soy sauce

$^1/_3$ cup salted peanuts

Hot cooked rice, preferably jasmine rice, for serving

PREP *Cut chicken breast into strips about 2 inches long and $^1/_2$ inch wide. Cut out and discard membrane and seeds of red pepper; cut pepper into $^1/_2$-inch dice. Thinly slice shallot crosswise; you should have about $^1/_3$ cup. Cut jalapeño into thin rings; do not remove seeds.*

1. Heat 1 tablespoon oil in large skillet over high heat. Add chicken and cook, stirring almost constantly, until lightly browned and cooked through, about 5 minutes. Transfer chicken to a plate.

2. Add remaining tablespoon oil to skillet and heat over high heat. Add red pepper and jalapeño and cook, stirring almost constantly, until red pepper begins to soften, about 1 minute. Add shallot and stir until it softens, about 30 seconds.

3. Return chicken to skillet. Add basil and soy sauce. Cook, stirring almost constantly, until basil wilts, about 1 minute. Stir in peanuts. Serve hot, spooned over the rice.

4 SERVINGS

other ideas

SIMPLE TIP *Many markets now carry bags of washed basil leaves. If you are using basil from a bunch, pluck the basil leaves from the stems. Place them in a large bowl of cold water to loosen any grit. Lift the leaves from the water, leaving any grit behind in the bottom of the bowl, and place them in a salad spinner. Give the leaves a few whirls in the spinner to dry them.*

DRESS IT UP *If you live near an Asian market, or if your supermarket carries Asian groceries (as many do), make the following changes:*

Substitute Thai fish sauce for the soy sauce.

Substitute Thai basil (also known as holy basil) for the regular basil.

Substitute a small Thai chile for the jalapeño.

VARIATION *Add 2 garlic cloves, thinly sliced, to the skillet with the shallots.*

Chicken Breasts with Vegetable Couscous

Quick-cooking couscous is truly a boon to the busy cook. In this dish, it's cooked in the skillet that cooked the chicken and vegetables, the better to soak up any flavorful juices left behind.

2 medium carrots

4 scallions

2 garlic cloves

1 pound boneless and skinless chicken breasts

2 tablespoons olive oil

One 15- to 19-ounce can garbanzo beans (chickpeas), drained and rinsed

1 teaspoon ground cumin

Hot cooked couscous, for serving

PREP *Cut carrots into $1/2$-inch dice. Slice scallions (white and green parts) into thin rounds. Finely chop garlic. Cut chicken breasts into strips about 2 inches long and $1/2$ inch wide.*

1 Heat 1 tablespoon olive oil in large skillet over medium heat. Add carrot and $1/4$ cup water. Cover and cook, stirring often, until carrots are crisp-tender and water evaporates, about 3 minutes. Add garbanzo beans, scallions, and garlic. Cook, stirring often, until scallions are wilted, about 2 minutes more. Transfer to plate.

2 Heat remaining tablespoon olive oil in skillet. Season chicken with $1/2$ teaspoon salt

and $1/4$ teaspoon freshly ground pepper. Add to skillet and cook, stirring often, until chicken is lightly browned and cooked through, about 6 minutes. Return vegetables to skillet. Add cumin and mix well. Add $1^1/2$ cups water and bring to boil, scraping up browned bits in skillet with wooden spatula.

3   To serve, spoon couscous into individual bowls. Top with chicken and vegetables and a spoonful of broth.

4 SERVINGS

other ideas

SIMPLE TIP *This skillet recipe illustrates another trick I have for simplified cooking. Sautéed meats and poultry will leave a thin layer of caramelized juices (called* fond *by chefs) in the bottom of the skillet. When these juices are mixed with the recipe's liquid, they become a light broth that can often replace canned or homemade broth.*

DRESS IT UP *Top each serving with chopped fresh cilantro.*

VARIATIONS *Season the liquid in the skillet with harissa (a Moroccan hot condiment made from red chiles and other spices, found at grocers with Mediterranean foods), or use an American hot red pepper sauce, such as Tabasco.*

Cook 1 red bell pepper, seeds and ribs discarded and flesh cut into $1/2$-inch dice, along with the carrots.

Chicken-Mushroom Fricassée with Tarragon

Fricassée conjures up images of old-fashioned boardinghouse meals and matronly cooks in gingham aprons, but this quick version of the farmhouse favorite is anything but stodgy. Tarragon is one of the first herbs to pop up in the spring garden, and it's put to good use here as a fragrant and flavorful accent. I love the simplicity of this no-frills recipe, but there are plenty of ways to jazz it up. You could serve it on egg noodles, or pass a basket full of freshly baked biscuits.

1 pound boneless and skinless chicken breasts

4 tablespoons ($\frac{1}{2}$ stick) butter

1 pound cremini (baby portobello) or white button mushrooms

$\frac{1}{3}$ cup finely chopped shallots (about 2 shallots)

$\frac{1}{4}$ cup all-purpose flour

2 teaspoons chopped fresh tarragon, or 1 teaspoon dried

2 cups milk, heated

Hot cooked egg noodles, for serving

PREP *Cut chicken breasts into 1-inch pieces.*

1 Melt 2 tablespoons butter in large skillet over medium-high heat. Season chicken with $\frac{1}{2}$ teaspoon salt and $\frac{1}{4}$ teaspoon freshly ground pepper. Add chicken to skil-

let and cook, stirring occasionally, until lightly browned on all sides, about 5 minutes. Transfer to a plate.

2 Heat remaining 2 tablespoons butter in skillet. Add mushrooms and cook, stirring often, until their juices evaporate, about 10 minutes. Add shallots and cook until they soften, about 2 minutes. Sprinkle with flour and tarragon and mix well. Stir in milk and bring to simmer.

3 Return chicken to skillet. Reduce heat to medium-low and simmer until chicken shows no sign of pink when pierced with a knife, about 10 minutes. Season with salt and pepper to taste. Spoon over noodles and serve.

4 TO 6 SERVINGS

other ideas

SIMPLE TIP *Every kitchen should have shallots, just as most have onions and garlic. Shallots look like very small red onions, and have a similar flavor, but because they're stronger than onions, you can use less. One average-size shallot, which contains two lobes under the papery brown skin, will yield about 3 tablespoons chopped shallot.*

DRESS IT UP *Add 1/2 cup chopped roasted red peppers and/or 1 cup thawed frozen peas to the fricassée during the last 5 minutes of cooking.*

Stir in 1/2 cup freshly grated Parmesan cheese.

VARIATIONS *Substitute 1 cup chicken broth for an equal amount of milk.*

Add 3 tablespoons dry sherry to the skillet with the milk; substitute chopped fresh parsley for the tarragon (do not use dried parsley).

Chicken and Sugar Snap Pea Stir-Fry with Creamy Pesto Sauce

When it comes to stir-fries, think outside of the box, as this Asian cooking method can be applied to Western flavors with great success. This one, with chicken and sweet sugar snap peas, is such a dish, with soy sauce nowhere in sight.

10 ounces sugar snap peas

1 pound boneless and skinless chicken breasts

2 tablespoons vegetable oil

2 teaspoons cornstarch

1 1/2 cups chicken broth

3 tablespoons pesto

3 tablespoons heavy cream

Hot cooked rice, for serving

PREP *Trim and remove strings from peas. Cut chicken into strips about 2 inches long and 1/2 inch wide.*

1 Heat very large skillet over medium-high heat until skillet is hot. Add 1 tablespoon oil and swirl to coat bottom of skillet. Add sugar snap peas and stir-fry until peas are crisp-tender, about 1 1/2 minutes. Transfer to plate.

2 Add remaining tablespoon oil to skillet and heat. Season chicken with $1/2$ teaspoon salt and $1/4$ teaspoon freshly ground pepper. Add to skillet and cook, stirring often, until chicken is lightly browned and almost cooked through, about 4 minutes. Return peas to skillet.

3 Sprinkle cornstarch over broth in small bowl and whisk to dissolve cornstarch. Pour into skillet. Stir in pesto and heavy cream. Cook until sauce comes to a boil and thickens, about 2 minutes. Season with salt and pepper to taste. Serve, spooned over rice.

4 SERVINGS

other ideas

SIMPLE TIP *My refrigerator is rarely without a container of store-bought prepared pesto. Just a spoonful adds fragrant zest to so many foods. To store leftover pesto, pour a thin film of olive oil over the top, cover, and refrigerate for up to 2 weeks.*

VARIATION *Substitute $1/4$ cup chopped fresh basil for the pesto.*

Mexican Chicken and Rice

Known as *arroz con pollo,* this skillet supper must feed millions of Latino diners every day, and for every good reason that makes a recipe popular. You will probably learn to cook it by memory, too, and often.

1 link smoked chorizo sausage

1 medium onion

1 red bell pepper

1 tablespoon olive oil

4 chicken breasts halves with skin and bone, about 10 ounces each

1 $^1/_4$ cups long-grain rice

1 cup thawed frozen peas

PREP *Cut chorizo into $^1/_2$-inch pieces. Chop onion. Cut off and discard seeds and ribs from pepper; cut pepper into $^1/_2$-inch dice.*

1 Heat olive oil in 9- to 10-inch-deep skillet over medium heat. Add chicken breasts, skin side down, and cook to brown the skin, about 3 minutes. Turn and brown the other sides, about 3 minutes more. Transfer to a plate.

2 Pour off all but 1 tablespoon of fat from the skillet. Add chorizo and cook until beginning to brown, about 3 minutes. Add onion and red pepper, and cook until veg-

etables soften, about 3 minutes. Stir in rice. Add 2 $1/2$ cups water, $1/2$ teaspoon salt, and $1/4$ teaspoon freshly ground pepper. Bring to boil, stirring up browned bits in bottom of pan. Return chicken to skillet and cover tightly.

3 Reduce heat to medium-low and simmer until rice is almost tender, about 25 minutes. Scatter peas over chicken, cover, and cook until rice has absorbed all liquid, about 5 minutes more. Remove from heat and let stand 5 minutes. Serve hot.

4 SERVINGS

other ideas

DRESS IT UP Arroz con pollo *is usually tinted yellow. To accomplish this look, which is optional in my kitchen, stir in* $1/4$ *teaspoon crushed saffron threads or* $1/2$ *teaspoon turmeric with the water.*

VARIATIONS *Add 2 garlic cloves to the skillet along with the onion and red pepper.*

Substitute 2 ounces smoked ham or 1 ounce pepperoni for the chorizo.

Use one 10-ounce box thawed frozen artichoke hearts instead of the peas.

If you have it, use chicken broth instead of the water.

Salami, Broccoli, and Red Pepper Frittata

Every cook should know how to make a frittata because the basic recipe can be altered with ingredients on hand to make almost endless variations. This time, I use salami to provide the backbone flavor, with roasted red pepper as an accent and broccoli (yes, thawed frozen, because its tenderness is perfect in this setting) for color.

2 scallions

1 tablespoon olive oil

3 ounces Genoa salami, cut into $1/4$-inch strips

One 10-ounce box thawed frozen chopped broccoli, **patted completely dry with paper towels**

$1/2$ cup drained and chopped roasted red pepper

8 large eggs

PREP *Slice scallions (white and green parts) into thin rounds.*

1 Position broiler rack 6 inches from source of heat and preheat broiler. Heat olive oil in 9- to 10-inch ovenproof, nonstick skillet over medium heat. Add salami and cook, stirring occasionally, until salami is lightly browned, about 4 minutes. Add scallions and cook until wilted, about 2 minutes. Add broccoli and red pepper and cook, stirring often, to evaporate excess moisture, about 2 minutes.

2 Whisk eggs, $3/4$ teaspoon salt, and $1/4$ teaspoon freshly ground pepper in medium bowl until uniformly yellow. Pour into skillet. Cook until edges begin to set, about 1 minute. Using heatproof silicone spatula, lift the set edge, allowing uncooked eggs to flow underneath the frittata. Continue cooking, occasionally lifting frittata with spatula as edges set, until frittata is mostly set.

3 Transfer skillet to broiler and cook until frittata is puffed and golden brown, about 1 minute. Slide out of skillet onto plate. Serve hot or cool to room temperature, cut into wedges.

4 TO 6 SERVINGS

other ideas

SIMPLE TIP *If you have any doubts about the flame resistance of your skillet's handle, wrap it in aluminum foil before placing it under the broiler.*

VARIATION *Substitute prosciutto, cut into $1/4$-inch dice, for the salami.*

Filet Mignon with Cremini Stroganoff

Any time that a recipe has filet mignon, the market receipt will be somewhat higher. No other cut of beef can match it for tenderness, so it's worthwhile splurging for an occasional treat. The filets are browned in a skillet, then kept warm in the oven (suspending them on a rack keeps them from giving off too many juices) while the mushrooms are sautéed. Because the steaks' internal temperature will rise a few degrees in the oven, don't overcook them at the browning stage—they'll end up a perfect medium-rare.

1 tablespoon vegetable oil

4 filets mignon, about 6 ounces each

20 ounces cremini (baby portobello) mushrooms, thinly sliced

$1/3$ cup finely chopped shallots

2 teaspoons sweet paprika, preferably Hungarian

$1^1/2$ cups sour cream

1 teaspoon cornstarch

Hot cooked noodles, for serving

1   Preheat oven to 200°F. Place a wire cake rack on a rimmed baking sheet. Heat oil in skillet over medium-high heat. Season beef with $1/2$ teaspoon salt and $1/4$ teaspoon

pepper. Place in skillet and cook until undersides are browned, about 2 $1/2$ minutes. Turn and cook to brown other sides, about 2 $1/2$ minutes more for medium-rare meat or longer if desired. Transfer fillets to cake rack and keep warm in oven while sautéing mushrooms.

2   Add mushrooms to pan juices in skillet and cook over medium-high heat, stirring occasionally, until mushrooms begin to brown, about 5 minutes. Add shallots and cook until they soften, about 1 minute. Stir in paprika.

3   Whisk sour cream and cornstarch together in small bowl to dissolve cornstarch. Stir into skillet and bring to a bare simmer, about 1 minute. Season with salt and pepper. Serve fillets with mushroom sauce and hot noodles.

4 SERVINGS

other ideas

SIMPLE TIP *Fermented dairy products, such as sour cream and yogurt, will curdle if heated above a simmer—that's why many recipes say only to warm them through without boiling when added to hot ingredients. A bit of cornstarch will stabilize the sour cream or yogurt, so it can be thoroughly heated without turning into a curdled mess.*

DRESS IT UP *Use an assortment of wild and cultivated mushrooms in addition to or instead of the cremini mushrooms. Stemmed shiitake caps would be sensational.*

VARIATION *Add 1 red bell pepper, ribs and seeds discarded, cut into $1/2$-inch dice, to the skillet along with the mushrooms.*

Ham and Artichoke Jambalaya

Many recipes for jambalaya call for simmering the rice in a tomato sauce, which is a sure way to a sticky disaster. To side-step disaster, cook the rice and spicy sauce separately, then mix just before serving.

1 medium onion

3 celery stalks

Two 6-ounce jars marinated artichokes, drained

1 cup long-grain rice

1 tablespoon vegetable oil

1 pound smoked ham, cut into bite-size chunks

2 teaspoons Cajun seasoning

One 28-ounce can chopped tomatoes in juice

PREP *Chop onion. Chop celery into $1/2$-inch dice. Coarsely chop artichokes.*

1 Bring 2 cups water and $1/2$ teaspoon salt to boil in $11/2$- to 2-quart saucepan over medium heat. Add rice and cover tightly. Reduce heat to low and simmer until rice has absorbed liquid and is tender, about 20 minutes. Let stand for 5 minutes.

2 Meanwhile, heat oil in large skillet. Add ham and cook until browned, about 5 minutes. Add onion and celery and cook, stirring occasionally, until onion is translucent, about 5 minutes. Add Cajun seasoning and stir for 15 seconds. Stir in tomatoes with

their juices and bring to a simmer. Reduce heat to low and simmer, stirring occasionally, until tomato juices thicken, about 20 minutes. Stir in artichokes.

3 Off heat, stir rice into tomato sauce. Serve hot.

4 SERVINGS

other ideas

SIMPLE TIP *When cooking rice, choose the right pot and you'll avoid a boiled-over mess (or conversely, rice that absorbs all of the liquid before it is tender). Rice triples in volume when cooked, and 1 cup raw rice will expand to 3 cups cooked. So, for that amount choose a 1 1/2-quart (6-cup) pot to allow for foaming and expansion, and you'll be fine. For more rice, use progressively larger saucepans.*

VARIATION *For chicken and artichoke jambalaya, substitute 1 pound boneless and skinless chicken breast, cut into 1-inch pieces, for the ham.*

Lamb Chops with Eggplant Ragù

Eggplant and lamb are such good companions; I have two recipes in this book that celebrate their friendship (see Moussaka with Roasted Eggplant on page 76). Here, lamb chops are simmered in an herb-scented mix of eggplant, tomatoes, onion, and garlic, with flavors that blend perfectly. If you want a starchy component, serve this with orzo.

1 medium eggplant, about 1 1/2 pounds

1 medium onion

2 garlic cloves

4 tablespoons olive oil

1 1/2 teaspoons herbes de Provence, store-bought or homemade
    (see *Simple Tip,* page 59)

4 leg of lamb chops, 8 ounces each

One 14 1/2-ounce can chopped tomatoes in juice

PREP *Trim eggplant and cut into 1-inch cubes. Chop onion. Finely chop garlic.*

1 Heat 3 tablespoons olive oil in a large nonstick skillet over high heat until oil is hot but not smoking. Add eggplant and cook, stirring often, until lightly browned, about 10 minutes. Move eggplant to one side of skillet. Add onion to empty area of skillet

and cook until softened, about 3 minutes. Add garlic and stir into onion until it gives off its aroma, about 1 minute. Transfer vegetables to plate.

2   Wipe out skillet. Heat remaining tablespoon olive oil over medium-high heat. Mix $3/4$ teaspoon herbes de Provence, $1/2$ teaspoon salt, and $1/4$ teaspoon pepper in small bowl. Season lamb chops with herb mixture. Add to skillet and cook, turning once, until browned on both sides, about 5 minutes. Transfer to serving platter.

3   Return vegetables to skillet, and stir in tomatoes with juices and remaining $3/4$ teaspoon herbes de Provence. Bring to a boil, scraping up browned bits in skillet with wooden spatula. Reduce heat to medium-low and cover tightly. Simmer 15 minutes. Return lamb and juices on platter to skillet, cover, and cook until lamb is medium-rare, about 5 minutes more. Season vegetables with salt and pepper to taste. Serve hot.

4 SERVINGS

other ideas

SIMPLE TIP *Eggplant soaks up cooking fat, making it difficult to cook—it can burn before it's cooked through and tender. If you aren't using a nonstick skillet, add more oil as needed to avoid scorching as the eggplant browns. Don't be surprised if you add quite a bit.*

DRESS IT UP *After returning the lamb to the skillet, sprinkle the lamb and ragù with 2 ounces (about $1/2$ cup) crumbled goat cheese (chèvre).*

VARIATION *Add 1 medium zucchini, cut into $1/2$-inch dice, to the skillet during the last 5 minutes of cooking the eggplant.*

Smothered Smoked Pork Chops with Kale and Hominy

Pork and greens have a special affinity for each other, and this dish shows off their compatibility beautifully. Look for smoked pork chops at Eastern European butchers and many supermarkets. Avoid the thin, boneless smoked chops, which aren't very meaty.

1 medium onion

4 garlic cloves

2 pounds curly kale, tough stems removed and leaves well rinsed

2 tablespoons vegetable oil

4 smoked pork chops, each cut 1 inch thick, about 7 ounces each

2 tablespoons cider vinegar

$1/4$ teaspoon crushed red pepper flakes

One 15-ounce can hominy, drained and rinsed

PREP *Chop onion. Chop garlic. Cut kale crosswise into $1/2$-inch shreds (see* Simple Tip*).*

1 Heat 1 tablespoon oil in very large skillet over medium-high heat. Season pork chops with $1/4$ teaspoon freshly ground pepper. Add to skillet and cook, turning once, until browned on both sides, about 5 minutes. Transfer chops to a plate.

2 Add remaining tablespoon oil to skillet and heat. Add onion and cook, stirring often,

until translucent, about 3 minutes. Stir in garlic and cook until it gives off its aroma, about 30 seconds. Add $1/2$ cup water, and scrape up browned bits in skillet. A handful at a time, stir in kale, waiting for first batch to wilt before adding more. Stir in vinegar and red pepper flakes and cover tightly.

3   Reduce heat to medium-low. Simmer for 20 minutes. Add hominy. Continue cooking until kale is tender and pork shows no sign of pink when pierced at the bone, about 20 minutes more. Serve hot.

4 SERVINGS

other ideas

SIMPLE TIP *Your supermarket may carry bags of washed, shredded kale, which are very convenient. To prepare kale yourself, cut off and discard the thick stems from the leaves. Fill a sink with lukewarm water. Add the kale and agitate the leaves to dislodge any grit. Lift the kale out of the water, leaving the grit on the bottom of the sink. Do not dry the kale—the clinging water will create steam in the skillet. A few at a time, stack the kale leaves and cut crosswise into $1/2$-inch-wide shreds.*

Pork Tenderloin and Bell Pepper Stir-Fry

Pork tenderloin is a popular ingredient in fast recipes. However, it can be bland, and can be enhanced with bold seasonings, as I have done here with a pile of peppers, along with balsamic vinegar, tomato paste, and oregano. Spoon it over hot rice to collect all of the tasty sauce.

3 bell peppers (preferably 1 each red, yellow, and orange)

2 garlic cloves

1 pound pork tenderloin

2 tablespoons olive oil

1 teaspoon dried oregano

2 tablespoons balsamic vinegar

2 teaspoons tomato paste

Hot cooked rice, for serving

PREP *Cut out and discard the ribs and seeds of peppers; cut peppers lengthwise into $1/4$-inch strips. Finely chop garlic.*

1 Using a sharp knife, cut tenderloin on a slight diagonal into $1/2$-inch-thick slices. Using a meat pounder or the heel of your hand, pound slices to $1/4$-inch thickness. Season pork with $1/2$ teaspoon salt and $1/4$ teaspoon freshly ground pepper.

2   Heat 1 tablespoon olive oil over medium heat. In batches, add pork and cook, turning once, until pork is browned on both sides, about 4 minutes. Transfer pork to a plate. Add remaining tablespoon olive oil to skillet and heat. Add peppers and garlic. Cook, stirring occasionally with a wooden spatula to loosen the browned bits in the skillet, until vegetables are tender, about 10 minutes. Return pork to the skillet and sprinkle with oregano. Cook, stirring occasionally, until pork is opaque throughout, about 2 minutes.

3   Mix $1/2$ cup water with balsamic vinegar and tomato paste to dissolve tomato paste. Stir into skillet, bring to a boil, and cook reduced by half, about 1 minute. Serve hot, spooned over the rice.

4 SERVINGS

other ideas

SIMPLE TIP *Here's the easiest way to prep bell peppers. Cut off the top half-inch or so of the pepper, including the stem, to make a "lid." Poke out the stem and discard it. Cut off the bottom half-inch of the pepper (it will look like a little cup) so it can stand on the counter. Make a lengthwise cut down the side of the pepper. Open up the pepper, and slice out the membrane with the seeds. You now have a long, wide strip of pepper, along with the top lid and the bottom cup. All of these pieces are ready to slice, dice, cut, or chop any way you wish.*

VARIATIONS *Add 1 medium red onion, thinly sliced into half-moons, to the skillet with the red peppers.*

This skillet supper is also delicious served over a mound of hot soft polenta.

Huge Potato Cake with Smoked Fish and Sour Cream

You'll be glad that you know how to make this golden, impressively large potato pancake. As a base for your favorite smoked fish and a dab of sour cream, it is hard to beat. But you'll also think of other ways to show it off—poached eggs and bacon, anyone?

2 pounds baking potatoes, such as Burbank or russet

1 small onion

1 large egg, beaten

2 tablespoons plain dry bread crumbs

5 tablespoons vegetable oil

$^3/_4$ cup sour cream, at room temperature

6 ounces thinly sliced cured smoked salmon, such as nova

1 Preheat oven to 400°F. Shred half of potatoes in food processor fitted with shredding disk. Shred onion onto potatoes. Shred remaining potatoes. Squeeze excess liquid from potato-onion mixture, one handful at a time. Transfer to medium bowl. Add egg, bread crumbs, $^1/_2$ teaspoon salt, and $^1/_4$ teaspoon freshly ground pepper and mix well.

2 Heat 3 tablespoons oil in 9- to 10-inch ovenproof nonstick skillet. Spread potato mixture in skillet. Cook until underside is lightly browned, about 5 minutes. Place large

flat lid or plate over skillet and invert lid and skillet together to turn potato cake onto lid. Add remaining 2 tablespoons oil to skillet and heat. Slide potato cake off lid back into skillet. Cook until other side browns, about 3 minutes.

3   Bake until potato cake looks cooked through when pierced in center with a knife, about 30 minutes. Slide out of skillet onto plate. Cut into wedges. Top each wedge with a dollop of sour cream and equal amounts of smoked salmon and serve.

6 SERVINGS

other ideas

DRESS IT UP *Top each serving with chopped fresh chives.*

VARIATION *In the Pacific Northwest, where I live, you can find fresh-smoked salmon, tuna, and other seafood at delicatessens and markets. Use any of these instead of the New York–style cured salmon, if you wish. You will use more of the fresh-smoked fish because it won't be thinly sliced.*

Sausages with Broccoli Rabe and White Beans

This satisfying Italian classic is just the thing for warming up an autumn evening. The slightly bitter edge of the broccoli rabe is balanced by the somewhat neutral beans. I prefer pork sausages, as they give off a reliable amount of flavorful juices to flavor the greens and beans, but the leaner turkey Italian sausages work well, too. Although it's more southern American than southern Italian, cornbread is the perfect sop for the cooking juices. Heated leftovers make a very nice pasta sauce—just chop the sausage, moisten the cooked pasta with a healthy splash of extra-virgin olive oil, and serve with lots of freshly grated Parmesan cheese.

8 links sweet Italian sausage with fennel, 1 1/2 pounds total

2 garlic cloves

1 large bunch broccoli rabe, about 1 1/4 pounds

1 tablespoon olive oil

One 15- to 19-ounce can white kidney (cannellini) beans, drained and rinsed

1/2 cup chicken broth

1/4 teaspoon crushed red pepper flakes

PREP *Pierce each sausage link in a few places with a sharp fork. Thinly slice garlic. Cut thick stems of broccoli rabe crosswise into $1/4$-inch-thick pieces; coarsely chop tops. Place broccoli rabe in sink of cold water and agitate to wash well. Drain in colander, but do not dry.*

1 Heat olive oil in large skillet over medium-high heat. Add sausage and cook, turning occasionally, until browned on all sides, about 5 minutes. Transfer sausage to a plate, leaving fat in skillet.

2 Reduce heat under skillet to medium. Add garlic and stir until it gives off its aroma, about 1 minute; do not brown. Add handfuls of broccoli rabe with clinging water to skillet, stirring until each batch wilts before adding more. Stir in beans, broth, and red pepper flakes. Bury sausages in greens.

3 Reduce heat to medium-low and cover tightly. Simmer until greens are very tender, about 30 minutes. Serve, with the cooking juices, in soup bowls.

4 SERVINGS

other ideas

SIMPLE TIP *Broccoli rabe looks like long-stemmed broccoli but is actually a mildly bitter green. It is sometimes labeled "broccoli rape" or "rapini," especially in neighborhoods with a large Italian clientele. Don't confuse it with broccolini, which has thinner stems.*

Cajun Shrimp Gumbo Sauté

The spicy taste of Cajun cooking is celebrated in this easy skillet dish. *Gumbo* means "okra" in Bantu African dialect, so not to include it is considered sacrilegious by many cooks. Don't turn your nose up at the okra, as it not only flavors the sauce but thickens it as well.

2 celery stalks

8 ounces fresh okra

4 scallions

1 $1/2$ pounds medium (26–30 count) shrimp

1 tablespoon olive oil

1 tablespoon salt-free Cajun seasoning

One 14 $1/2$-ounce can chopped tomatoes in juice

Hot cooked rice, for serving

PREP *Chop celery into $1/2$-inch dice. Trim off and discard caps from okra; slice okra crosswise into $1/4$-inch-thick rounds. Chop white and green parts of scallions. Peel and devein shrimp.*

1 Heat olive oil in large skillet over medium heat. Add celery and cook until it begins to soften, about 2 minutes. Add okra and scallions and cook until scallions wilt, about 2 minutes.

2 Sprinkle vegetables with Cajun seasoning and stir for 15 seconds. Stir in tomatoes with juice and 1 cup water. Bring to boil. Reduce heat to low, cover tightly, and simmer until well flavored, about 20 minutes.

3 Stir in shrimp and increase heat to medium. Simmer until shrimp turn opaque and firm, about 3 minutes. Season with salt. Serve hot, spooned over hot rice.

4 TO 6 SERVINGS

other ideas

SIMPLE TIP *There is no standard for shrimp size. One locale's large is another's jumbo. The best way to choose your shrimp is by the number of pieces per pound, which is usually shown on the label or sign. Generally, 21 to 25 shrimp to a pound designates large shrimp.*

DRESS IT UP *Sauté $1/2$ chopped ($1/2$-inch dice) red bell pepper with the celery.*

Add 2 garlic cloves, finely chopped, to the skillet along with the okra and scallions.

Use 1 cup bottled clam juice instead of the water.

VARIATION *Substitute 1 pound crab meat, picked over for shells and cartilage, for the shrimp.*

Snapper Fillets with Zucchini and Grape Tomatoes

Fish should be cooked quickly to retain its texture and flavor, so if you're cooking against the clock, head to the fish counter at the market. This fresh-tasting sauté of zucchini and grape tomatoes is a fine match for the delicate fish.

3 medium zucchini, well scrubbed

1 garlic clove

1 pint grape tomatoes

2 tablespoons olive oil

$1/3$ cup pitted and chopped Kalamata olives

$1 1/2$ teaspoons herbes de Provence (see *Simple Tip,* page 59), or $1/2$ teaspoon
   each thyme, basil, and crumbled dried rosemary

4 snapper fillets, about 6 ounces each

Lemon wedges, for serving

PREP *Cut zucchini in half lengthwise, then into $1/4$-inch-thick rounds. Finely chop garlic. Cut tomatoes in half lengthwise with small serrated knife.*

1 Heat 1 tablespoon olive oil in large nonstick skillet over medium-high heat. Add zucchini and cook, stirring occasionally, until zucchini is browned and tender, about 12 minutes. Stir in garlic and cook until garlic gives off its aroma, about 1 minute. Stir in

tomatoes, olives, and $^3/_4$ teaspoon herbes de Provence. Cook, stirring occasionally, until tomatoes are heated through still holding their shape, about 3 minutes. Season with salt and pepper to taste. Transfer to rimmed serving platter and cover with aluminum foil to keep warm.

2   Add remaining tablespoon oil to skillet and heat over medium-high heat. Mix $^3/_4$ teaspoon herbes de Provence, $^1/_4$ teaspoon salt, and $^1/_4$ teaspoon freshly ground pepper in small bowl. Season snapper fillets with herb mixture. Place fillets in skillet, skin side up, and cook until underside is browned, about 3 minutes. Turn and cook until fillets are barely opaque when flaked in thickest part with tip of a knife, about 3 minutes more.

3   Top ragù with fish fillets and serve hot, with lemon wedges.

4 SERVINGS

other ideas

SIMPLE TIP *Many markets now carry pitted Kalamata olives, but unpitted olives can be pitted without any special equipment. Hold a large knife or cleaver parallel to and just above the work surface. Place an olive under the flat, wide part of the knife. Using your fist, hit the knife above the olive, just to crush the olive. The pit is now easy to remove. Don't worry that the olive is crushed, because you are going to chop it, anyway.*

VARIATION *Any firm-fleshed fish fillets, from sea bass to grouper, can stand in for the snapper.*

Sesame Tuna Steak on Napa Cabbage

Crusted with a sprinkle of sesame seeds, and served on a quick sauté of napa cabbage, this dish has an elegant simplicity that gives it almost restaurant sophistication. It's seasoned with ponzu, a flavored soy sauce that is making its way into local supermarkets.

1 pound napa cabbage

2 large carrots

2 scallions

1 tablespoon vegetable oil

1 tablespoon shredded fresh ginger (use the large holes of a box grater)

2 tablespoons ponzu, plus more for serving

4 boneless tuna steaks, about 6 ounces each

2 tablespoons sesame seeds

PREP *Cut cabbage in half, and cut out core. Cut cabbage crosswise into thin slices. Shred carrots on large holes of box grater. Slice white and green parts of scallions into thin rounds, keeping them separate.*

1 Heat oil in large nonstick skillet over medium-high heat. Add ginger and stir until it softens, about 15 seconds. A handful at a time, add cabbage, letting first batch wilt before adding more. Add carrots, white parts of scallions, and 1/4 cup water. Cook until cabbage is tender, about 5 minutes. Stir in 2 tablespoons ponzu. Season with

salt and pepper to taste. Transfer to rimmed serving platter and cover with aluminum foil to keep warm.

2   Wipe out skillet. Heat empty skillet over medium-high heat. Season tuna with $1/4$ teaspoon salt and $1/4$ teaspoon freshly ground pepper. Sprinkle tuna on both sides with sesame seeds, pressing them to adhere. Place in skillet and cook until sesame seeds on underside turn golden, about 2 minutes. Turn and repeat with other side, about 2 minutes more.

3   Place tuna on cabbage and sprinkle with scallion greens. Serve hot, with 4 small bowls of ponzu for dipping tuna.

4 SERVINGS

other ideas

SIMPLE TIP *Ponzu—soy sauce flavored with citrus juice or rice vinegar, dried fish flakes, seaweed, and more—can be found in supermarkets' Asian section or next to the soy sauce in the condiments aisle. If you wish, substitute 2 tablespoons soy sauce and 1 tablespoon fresh lime juice or rice vinegar.*

VARIATION *Add 1 finely chopped garlic clove to the skillet with the ginger.*

the simpler the better # From the Pot: Stews, Ragùs, and Chilies

Tuscan Beef Stew

Italian cooks are famous for cooking creatively and deliciously with a handful of ingredients. This stew is typical of Tuscany, where many dishes include the local red wine. Don't bother opening up a bottle of fine Chianti for cooking—moderately priced American or Australian wine will do. Serve it over hot polenta or small pasta, such as ditalini.

3 ounces pancetta, sliced about $1/4$ inch thick

1 medium onion

2 celery stalks

1 tablespoon olive oil

3 pounds boneless beef chuck, cut into 1-inch pieces

1 cup hearty red wine, such as Sangiovese, Zinfandel, or Shiraz

One 28-ounce can crushed tomatoes in puree

$1/4$ cup chopped fresh basil

PREP *Cut pancetta into $1/4$- to $1 1/2$-inch dice. Chop onion. Chop celery crosswise into $1/4$-inch-thick slices.*

1   Combine pancetta and olive oil in Dutch oven and cook, stirring occasionally, until pancetta browns, about 5 minutes. Using slotted spoon, transfer pancetta to plate. Season beef with 1 teaspoon salt and $1/2$ teaspoon freshly ground pepper. Increase

heat to medium-high. In batches, add to fat in pot and cook, turning occasionally, until browned, about 5 minutes. Transfer to plate with pancetta.

2   Add onion and celery to pot. Reduce heat to medium and cook, stirring often, until vegetables soften, about 3 minutes. Add wine to pot, scraping up browned bits on bottom, and bring to boil. Return beef, pancetta, and any juices on plate to pot. Stir in tomatoes and bring to a boil. Reduce heat to medium-low and cover. Simmer until beef is tender, about 1 1/2 hours.

3   Stir in basil. Serve hot.

6 SERVINGS

other ideas

SIMPLE TIP *Pancetta is the same cut as bacon but rolled up into a cylinder and cured without smoke. You'll find it at many supermarkets and certainly all Italian delicatessens. Ask the deli person to slice it on the thick side, about 1/4 inch thick, and not paper thin, as is probably their habit. If you can't find it, use regular sliced bacon.*

Red Curry Beef with Potatoes

Here's another recipe that uses red curry paste, one of my favorite ingredients. In fact, it is probably the most famous use for red curry paste—a luxuriously spiced beef stew with chunks of potatoes.

2 large onions

1 1/2 pounds red-skinned potatoes

2 limes

3 tablespoons vegetable oil

2 pounds beef chuck, cut into 1-inch pieces

3 tablespoons red curry paste

Two 13 1/2-ounce cans coconut milk (do not shake cans)

3 tablespoons soy sauce or fish sauce

PREP *Cut onions into 1/2-inch-thick half-moons. Cut potatoes into 1/2-inch-thick rounds. Grate zest from limes. Juice limes; you should have 2 to 3 tablespoons.*

1   Heat 2 tablespoons oil in Dutch oven or flameproof covered casserole over medium-high heat. In batches without crowding, add beef and cook, turning occasionally, until beef is browned, about 5 minutes. Transfer beef to plate.

2   Heat remaining tablespoon oil in pot. Add onions and reduce heat to medium. Cook, stirring occasionally, until onions soften, about 5 minutes. Add curry paste and 2 tablespoons thick coconut "cream" (the thick liquid that has risen to the top of the

canned coconut milk). Mix well and cook for 30 seconds. Return beef and any juices on plate to pot. Whisk coconut milk in cans to combine milk and remaining "cream" and pour into pot, along with soy sauce. Bring to a boil. Reduce heat to medium-low. Cover and simmer for 50 minutes.

3 Add potatoes to pot and cover. Cook until both beef and potatoes are tender, about 35 minutes. Add lime zest and juice. Serve hot.

4 SERVINGS

other ideas

SIMPLE TIP *Don't confuse coconut milk with cream of coconut (such as Coco Lopez). The former is unsweetened, while the latter is used only for making piña coladas and some desserts. However, the thick, rich paste that rises to the top of canned coconut milk during storage is similarly called "coconut cream." The question is what to buy? The answer is coconut milk.*

VARIATION *Add 1 green bell pepper (seeds and ribs discarded, pepper cut into 2-inch long strips about $1/2$ inch wide) and 2 finely chopped garlic cloves to the pot with the onion.*

Texas Beef Chili

One can't have a book on one-pot meals without a solid chili recipe.

Texans will argue about the addition of beans or tomatoes to the pot,

but I say that anything goes, as long as it tastes as good as this.

1 large onion

2 garlic cloves

2 tablespoons olive oil

3 pounds beef chuck, cut into 1-inch pieces

1 tablespoon chili powder

Two 14 $1/2$-ounce cans chopped tomatoes with chiles, drained

One 12-ounce bottle lager beer

Two 15- to 19-ounce cans pinto beans, drained and rinsed

PREP *Chop onion. Finely chop garlic.*

1   Heat 1 tablespoon olive oil in Dutch oven or covered flameproof casserole over medium-high heat. Season beef with 1 teaspoon salt and $1/2$ teaspoon freshly ground pepper. In batches, add beef to pot and cook, stirring occasionally, until browned, about 5 minutes. Transfer to a plate.

2   Add remaining tablespoon olive oil to pot and heat. Add onion and cook, stirring often, until onion softens, about 3 minutes. Add garlic and cook until it gives off its aroma, about 1 minute. Add chili powder and stir for 15 seconds. Add tomatoes and

beer and bring to a boil, scraping up browned bits on bottom of pot. Return beef and juices on platter to pot and cover. Reduce heat to medium-low.

3   Simmer until beef is tender, about 1 1/2 hours. Add beans and cook until heated through, about 10 minutes. To thicken chili, crush some beans against side of pot with a large spoon. Season with salt and pepper to taste. Serve hot.

6 TO 8 SERVINGS

other ideas

SIMPLE TIP *Whenever cooking with spices, such as chili powder or curry powder, add the spices to the basic seasoning ingredients (usually cooked vegetables) and stir for a few seconds before adding any liquids. The essential oils in the spices will heat up when they come into contact with the pot (or skillet, or what have you) and release more flavor.*

DRESS IT UP *For toppings, serve bowls of any or all of the following: shredded Cheddar cheese, sour cream, pickled jalapeño rings, chopped scallions, sliced black olives.*

VARIATIONS *Add 1 jalapeño pepper, seeded and finely chopped, to the pot with the onion.*

Substitute 1 cup fresh or thawed frozen corn kernels for 1 can of beans.

Don't feel like using beer? Substitute 1 1/2 cups beef broth.

Hunter's Chicken

When Italians talk about food cooked *alla cacciatore,* the term implies a wild mushroom and tomato sauce. (*Cacciatore* means "hunter's style," and it is assumed that a hunter would bring home wild mushrooms as well as meat.) There's no need to gather wild mushrooms in the woods now that supermarkets carry full-flavored cremini mushrooms, which are domesticated but still tasty.

1 pound cremini (baby portobello) mushrooms

1 medium onion

2 tablespoons olive oil

1 large chicken, about 4 pounds, cut into 8 serving pieces

$1/2$ cup hearty red wine, such as Zinfandel or Shiraz

One 28-ounce can crushed tomatoes with puree

1 teaspoon Italian seasoning, or $1/2$ teaspoon each dried basil and oregano

Hot cooked polenta, for serving

PREP *Cut mushrooms into quarters. Chop onion.*

1 Heat olive oil in Dutch oven or covered flameproof casserole over medium-high heat. Season chicken with $1/2$ teaspoon salt and $1/4$ teaspoon freshly ground pepper. In batches, add chicken to pot and cook, turning occasionally, until browned, about 6 minutes. Transfer chicken to plate.

2 Pour off all but 1 tablespoon fat from pot. Add mushrooms and cook, stirring occasionally, until they give off their liquid, about 5 minutes. Add onion and cook, stirring occasionally, until mushrooms are tender, about 5 minutes more. Stir in wine, then crushed tomatoes and Italian seasoning. Bring to a boil, stirring up browned bits on bottom of pot. Return chicken to pot and cover. Reduce heat to medium-low.

3 Simmer until chicken shows no sign of pink when pierced near the bone, about 40 minutes. Season sauce with salt and pepper. Serve hot, spooned over hot polenta.

4 SERVINGS

other ideas

SIMPLE TIP *Instant polenta, which cooks up into a soft golden mound, is the Italian answer to mashed potatoes. It's just the thing to serve with saucy stews like this one. You'll find it at Italian delicatessens and in the pasta section of most supermarkets.*

Spanish Chicken and Garbanzo Stew

The flavors of Spain are making welcome inroads into American cooking. Spain is famous for its paprika, but if it isn't available in your area, look for sweet Hungarian paprika. Either of these imported spices will have much more oomph than the standard supermarket variety. And be sure to use dry, not sweet, sherry. You'll want to serve crusty bread with this one to sop up the brick-red juices.

2 medium onions

1 large red bell pepper

2 tablespoons olive oil

1 large chicken, about 4 pounds, cut into 8 serving pieces

1 tablespoon sweet paprika, preferably Spanish or Hungarian

$1/2$ cup dry sherry

Two 15- to 19-ounce cans garbanzo beans (chickpeas), drained and rinsed

PREP *Cut onions into $1/2$-inch-wide half-moons. Cut out and discard seeds and ribs from pepper; cut pepper into 2-inch-long strips about $1/2$ inch wide.*

1 Heat olive oil in Dutch oven or flameproof covered casserole over medium-high heat. In batches without crowding, add chicken. Cook, occasionally turning chicken, until lightly browned, about 5 minutes. Transfer chicken to plate.

2 Pour out all but 1 tablespoon fat from pot. Return pot to medium heat. Add onions and red pepper and cover. Cook, stirring occasionally, until vegetables soften, about 5 minutes. Return chicken to the pot, season with paprika and $1/2$ teaspoon salt, and mix well. Add sherry and bring to a boil. Reduce heat to medium-low and cover. Simmer until chicken shows no sign of pink when pierced at the bone, about 40 minutes. During last 10 minutes of cooking, stir in garbanzos.

3 To thicken sauce, mash some beans against side of pot with a large spoon. Serve hot in deep bowls.

4 SERVINGS

other ideas

DRESS IT UP Pimentón de la Vera, *oak-smoked paprika from the Spanish microclimate of La Vera, is increasingly available at specialty food stores. It you find it, use this wonderfully distinctive spice just like regular paprika, but brace yourself for a hearty dose of smokiness.*

VARIATION *Substitute 2 pounds of boneless pork loin (not tenderloin), cut into 1-inch pieces. Brown the pork in the oil and set aside, then proceed with the recipe. When simmering the pork, cook it for only 20 minutes, or until it is opaque throughout. Overcooking will dry out the pork.*

Cod and Calamari Cioppino

San Francisco is the home of cioppino, a zesty fish and shellfish stew. You'll often find it made with crab, but sweet (and shell-free) calamari is a quick-cooking and delicious substitute for the crustacean. Serve this with plenty of crusty sourdough bread.

1 medium onion

1 green bell pepper

2 garlic cloves

1 pound skinless cod fillets

6 ounces cleaned calamari

2 tablespoons olive oil

$1/2$ cup hearty red wine, such as Zinfandel or Shiraz

Two $14\,1/2$-ounce cans chopped tomatoes with Italian herbs

PREP *Chop onion. Cut off and discard seeds and ribs from green pepper; cut pepper into $1/2$-inch dice. Finely chop garlic. Cut cod into 1-inch pieces. Cut calamari crosswise into $1/4$-inch-wide rings. Coarsely chop calamari tentacles, if any.*

1 Heat olive oil in Dutch oven or covered flameproof casserole over medium-high heat. Add onion, bell pepper, and garlic and cook, stirring often, until onion is translucent, about 6 minutes.

2 Stir in red wine, then tomatoes with their juices, and 1 cup water. Bring to a boil. Reduce heat to low and partially cover pot. Simmer for 30 minutes.

3 Add cod and cook for 3 minutes. Add calamari and cook until it is tender and cod is cooked through, about 3 minutes more. Season with salt and pepper to taste. Ladle into bowls and serve hot.

4 SERVINGS

other ideas

SIMPLE TIP *For cooking, look for full-bodied red wines with a bit of acidity. Zinfandel and Shiraz are good choices, but Merlot may be too fruity and Beaujolais is a bit thin bodied.*

VARIATIONS *Leave out the red wine and use 1/2 cup bottled clam juice.*

Substitute 1/2 cup peeled and deveined medium shrimp (26–30 count) for calamari.

Season with crushed hot red pepper flakes instead of freshly ground pepper.

Cuban Pork Stew with Rice, Black Beans, and Cilantro

All over the Caribbean, but especially in Cuba, you'll find the combination of rice and black beans. With the addition of pork chunks, they become a hearty meal.

1 large onion

4 garlic cloves

2 tablespoons olive oil

3 pounds boneless pork loin (not tenderloin), cut into 1-inch pieces

2 1/2 cups chicken broth

1/2 cup long-grain rice

One 15- to 19-ounce can black beans, rinsed and drained

1/3 cup chopped fresh cilantro

PREP *Chop onion. Finely chop garlic.*

1 Heat 1 tablespoon olive oil in Dutch oven or covered flameproof casserole over medium-high heat. Season pork with 1 teaspoon salt and 1/4 teaspoon freshly ground pepper. In batches, add pork and cook, turning occasionally, until browned, about 6 minutes. Transfer pork to platter.

2 Heat remaining tablespoon olive oil in pot and reduce heat to medium. Add onion and cook until translucent, about 5 minutes. Add garlic and cook until it gives off its

aroma, about 1 minute. Return pork and juices on platter to pot, add broth, and bring to a boil. Stir in rice. Reduce heat to medium-low and partially cover pot. Simmer until pork is tender, about 1 hour.

3 Stir in beans and cilantro and cook until beans are cooked through, about 7 minutes. Season with salt and pepper to taste. To thicken sauce, crush some beans and rice against side of pot with a large spoon. Serve hot.

6 SERVINGS

other ideas

DRESS IT UP *Add ¹/₂ cup sliced pimiento-stuffed green olives to the stew along with the black beans.*

Country Ribs with Sauerkraut and Dried Apples

Thick and meaty country ribs have many uses off the barbecue grill. They can be simmered in stews, where their meat becomes tender while the bones add flavor to the cooking juices. Here's a great way to cook with country ribs indoors. I find that dried apples hold up in a stew better than fresh apples. If you wish, serve boiled new potatoes on the side.

1 large onion

2 garlic cloves

Three 1-pound bags refrigerated sauerkraut

8 meaty country ribs, 4 pounds total

1 tablespoon vegetable oil

1 teaspoon caraway seeds

One 12-ounce bottle hard apple cider

4 ounces dried apple slices

PREP *Chop onion. Finely chop garlic. Drain sauerkraut in colander. Rinse well under cold water and squeeze out excess liquid.*

1   Position broiler rack 6 inches from source of heat and preheat broiler. Season ribs with 1 teaspoon salt and $1/4$ teaspoon freshly ground pepper. Broil ribs, turning occasionally, until browned, about 10 minutes.

2   Heat oil in Dutch oven or covered flameproof casserole over medium heat. Add onion and cook, stirring often, until onion is golden, about 6 minutes. Add garlic and cook until it gives off its aroma, about 1 minute. Stir in caraway and cook for 30 seconds. Add sauerkraut, cider, and apples and mix well. Bury ribs in sauerkraut. Reduce heat to medium-low and cover.

3   Simmer until ribs are tender, about 1¼ hours. Season with salt and pepper to taste. Serve hot.

4 SERVINGS

other ideas

SIMPLE TIP *Made from fermented apple juice, and therefore alcoholic, hard apple cider is easily available in 12-ounce bottles at liquor stores. France is famous for its cider from Normandy, but there are many delicious domestic ciders, especially from northern New England.*

VARIATION *Substitute 1 cup semidry white wine, such as Riesling, for the apple cider. Or use regular apple juice.*

Braised Pork Pot Roast and Red Cabbage

Beef doesn't have a corner on the pot roast market. This braised pork roast is smothered in sweet-and-sour red cabbage and simmered to juicy tenderness.

1 large onion

1 red cabbage, about 2 $1/2$ pounds

2 tablespoons vegetable oil

$1/2$ teaspoon dried thyme

3 pounds boneless pork loin roast, tied

$1/3$ cup balsamic vinegar

$1/2$ cup red currant jelly

Hot cooked noodles, for serving

PREP *Chop onion. Cut cabbage into quarters; cut out core. Thinly slice cabbage crosswise.*

1 Heat 1 tablespoon oil in Dutch oven or covered flameproof casserole over medium-high heat. Mix thyme, $1/2$ teaspoon salt, and $1/4$ teaspoon freshly ground pepper and rub over pork. Add pork to pot and cook, turning occasionally, until browned on all sides, about 8 minutes. Transfer pork to plate.

2 Heat remaining tablespoon oil in pot and add onion. Reduce heat to medium and cook, stirring occasionally, until onion softens, about 3 minutes. In batches if neces-

sary, add cabbage to pot, sprinkling it with balsamic vinegar. Stir in jelly and $1/2$ cup water. Bury pork in cabbage. Reduce heat to medium-low and cover.

3   Simmer until cabbage is tender and meat thermometer inserted in center of roast reads 150°F, about 1 $1/4$ hours. Season cabbage with salt and pepper to taste. Remove pork from pot and cover cabbage to keep warm. Let pork stand 10 minutes. Carve and serve hot, with the noodles.

6 SERVINGS

other ideas

SIMPLE TIP *Red cabbage turns an odd color unless it is cooked with an acid. In this recipe, balsamic vinegar plays this role. Use a moderately priced brand, not the aged, artisan variety.*

DRESS IT UP *Add one 15-ounce jar vacuum-packed chestnuts, coarsely chopped, to the cabbage during the last 10 minutes of cooking.*

Lamb Shanks with Garlicky White Beans and Rosemary

Yes, lamb shanks do take a good amount of time to become tender, but once they reach that state of perfection, they will literally melt in your mouth. Although they shrink during cooking, the shanks will need a fairly large Dutch oven. It's all time well spent.

12 whole garlic cloves

2 tablespoons olive oil

4 lamb shanks, 1 pound each

$1/2$ cup dry white wine, such as Sauvignon Blanc

$1/2$ pound baby-cut carrots

One 15- to 19-ounce can white beans (cannellini), drained and rinsed

2 tablespoons chopped fresh rosemary, plus optional rosemary sprigs
    for garnish

PREP *Smash each garlic clove under flat, wide side of large knife; peel garlic.*

1   Heat 1 tablespoon olive oil in large Dutch oven over medium-high heat. Season lamb with 1 teaspoon salt and $1/2$ teaspoon freshly ground pepper. In batches, add to pot and cook, turning occasionally, until browned, about 5 minutes. Transfer shanks to plate. Pour out fat in pot.

2   Add remaining tablespoon olive oil to pot and heat. Add garlic and cook, stirring often, just until it gives off fragrance, about 1 minute. Add wine and $^1/_2$ cup water and bring to a boil, scraping up browned bits in pot. Return lamb to pot. Reduce heat to low and cover tightly. Cook at a bare simmer until lamb is almost tender, about 2 $^1/_2$ hours.

3   Add carrots to pot, then top with white beans and chopped rosemary. Cover again and continue cooking until lamb is very tender, about 30 minutes more. Stir carrots and beans to combine with rosemary and season with salt and pepper. To serve, spoon vegetables into 4 deep soup bowls and top each with a shank. Garnish each serving with a rosemary sprig, if desired.

4 SERVINGS

other ideas

SIMPLE TIP *For most recipes that call for white wine, a dry variety with a bit of acidity works best to balance the fat in the dish. Sauvignon Blanc and Pinot Grigio are two fine options.*

VARIATION *Do try to make this with fresh rosemary. But if you wish, substitute 2 teaspoons dried rosemary, added to the pot along with the lamb.*

Dubliner's Lamb Stew with Stout

Where I live, the weather on St. Patrick's Day is almost guaranteed to be chilly. But no matter how cold it gets, Irish stew, chock-full of lamb, potatoes, and carrots, is guaranteed to warm me up. It will do the trick for you, too. The secret ingredient here is dark, rich stout, with its slightly roasted flavor.

3 tablespoons vegetable oil

4 pounds lamb neck on the bone

1 large onion, chopped

$1/4$ cup all-purpose flour

One 12-ounce bottom stout, such as Guinness

$1 1/2$ pounds red-skinned or Yukon Gold potatoes

$1/2$ pound baby-cut carrots

2 tablespoons chopped fresh parsley

1   Preheat oven to 300°F. Heat 2 tablespoons oil in Dutch oven or covered flameproof casserole over medium-high heat. Season lamb with 1 teaspoon salt and $1/2$ teaspoon freshly ground pepper. In batches, add lamb to pot and cook, turning occasionally, until browned, about 6 minutes. Transfer lamb to plate.

2   Heat remaining tablespoon oil in pot. Add onion and cover. Cook until onion is translucent, scraping up browned bits on bottom of pan, about 5 minutes. Return

lamb to pot. Sprinkle with flour and mix well. Stir in 2 $1/2$ cups water and stout and bring to a boil.

3   Cover pot. Bake for 1 $1/4$ hours. Submerge potatoes and carrots in cooking liquid and cover again. Bake until lamb and vegetables are tender, about 45 minutes more. Season with salt and pepper to taste. Sprinkle with parsley and serve.

6 TO 8 SERVINGS

other ideas

SIMPLE TIP *The cut of choice for lamb stew is usually boneless shoulder, but it is getting increasingly difficult to find. Supermarkets are more likely to carry lamb neck on the bone, which is a mixed blessing. Lamb neck may have bones that are a little difficult to maneuver during eating, but those very bones release lots of flavor into the stew. I guess I don't miss lamb shoulder that much after all. If your butcher carries boneless lamb shoulder, and you care to use it, you'll need only 3 pounds. (All of this also applies to the veal neck used in Provençal Veal Stew on page 158.)*

New Orleans Hot Links with Red Beans and Rice

It was Louis Armstrong who used to sign his letters "Red beans and ricely, very much," which is about the best endorsement a recipe can ask for! Hot link sausages add just the right amount of spice.

1 pound hot link sausages

1 medium onion

1 green bell pepper

2 celery stalks

2 garlic cloves

2 tablespoons vegetable oil

Three 15- to 19-ounce cans small red beans, undrained

Hot cooked rice, for serving

PREP *Cut sausages into $1/2$-inch-thick rounds. Chop onion. Cut out and discard seeds and ribs from pepper; cut pepper into $1/2$-inch dice. Cut celery crosswise into $1/4$-inch-thick slices. Finely chop garlic.*

1 Heat oil in Dutch oven over medium heat. Add sausage and cook, stirring occasionally, until browned, about 5 minutes. Add onion, green pepper, celery, and garlic. Cover and cook, stirring occasionally, scraping up browned bits on bottom of pot. until vegetables soften, about 10 minutes. Add beans and their juices and 1 cup water. Bring to a boil.

2   Reduce heat to low and simmer to blend flavors, about 45 minutes. Season with salt and pepper.

3   To serve, spoon rice into bowls and top with beans.

6 SERVINGS

other ideas

VARIATIONS *For a milder pot of beans, substitute pork or turkey kielbasa for the hot links.*

For a spicier pot of beans, stir in 2 teaspoons salt-free Cajun seasoning to the cooked vegetables before adding the beans and their liquid.

Provençal Veal Stew

Herbes de Provence lend their perfume to this lovely stew. The bones in the veal neck flavor the cooking liquid, making the use of additional broth unnecessary (see *Simple Tip*, page 155).

3 garlic cloves

1 1/2 pounds red-skinned or Yukon Gold potatoes, scrubbed

4 tablespoons olive oil

4 pounds veal neck on the bone

1/4 cup all-purpose flour

1 1/2 teaspoons herbes de Provence (see *Simple Tip*, page 59), or 1/2 teaspoon
each dried basil, thyme, and rosemary

1/2 cup dry white wine, such as Sauvignon Blanc

1/2 pound baby-cut carrots

PREP *Finely chop garlic. Cut potatoes into 3/4-inch cubes.*

1 Preheat oven to 300°F. Heat 2 tablespoons olive oil in Dutch oven over medium-high heat. Season veal with 1 teaspoon salt and 1/2 teaspoon freshly ground pepper. In batches, add veal and cook, stirring occasionally, until browned, about 6 minutes. Transfer veal to plate.

2 Add remaining 2 tablespoons oil and heat. Add garlic and stir until garlic gives off its aroma, about 1 minute. Return veal and juices on plate to pot. Sprinkle with flour and

herbes de Provence and mix well. Stir in wine and 2 1/2 cups water, scraping up browned bits on bottom of pot.

3 Cover tightly. Bake for 1 hour. Add potatoes, pushing into cooking liquid, cover again, and bake for 15 minutes more. Add baby carrots, submerging into cooking liquid, and bake covered until veal and potatoes are tender, about 30 minutes more. Season with salt and pepper to taste. Serve hot.

6 SERVINGS

other ideas

SIMPLE TIP *Baking in a low oven prevents the stew's sauce from scorching on the bottom of the pot. However, you can simmer the stew on the stove as long as you use a Flametamer to keep the heat low.*

DRESS IT UP *Add 1/2 cup pitted and coarsely chopped Kalamata olives to the stew during the last 5 minutes of baking.*

Sprinkle chopped fresh parsley over each serving.

VARIATIONS *Use lamb neck instead of the veal for a nice change.*

Add 1 cup frozen baby onions, thawed, to the pot with the baby carrots.

Gnocchi with Asparagus, Mascarpone, and Prosciutto

Usually made from potatoes and flour, gnocchi are tender pillows of pasta. You'll find the imported vacuum-packed ones at your local Italian delicatessen, and maybe the supermarket, too. Mascarpone, that deliciously rich and buttery cheese, creates a spectacular sauce for this elegant dish.

1 $^1/_2$ pounds asparagus

One 1 $^1/_{10}$-pound vacuum-packed package Italian gnocchi

1 tablespoon butter

1 slice ($^1/_8$ inch thick) prosciutto, about 3 ounces

One 8-ounce container mascarpone, at room temperature

$^1/_2$ cup freshly grated Parmesan cheese

$^1/_2$ cup chopped fresh basil

PREP *Snap off and discard woody ends from asparagus. Cut spears into 1-inch lengths. Cut prosciutto into $^1/_4$-inch dice.*

1 Bring a large pot of lightly salted water to a boil over high heat. Add the asparagus and cook until barely tender, about 5 minutes. Using a skimmer or a wire strainer, transfer asparagus to a bowl. Gradually stir gnocchi into the same pot. Cook, stirring

occasionally, until the gnocchi are tender, about 8 minutes. Drain and set gnocchi aside. Do not rinse gnocchi.

2   Melt butter in the same pot over medium heat. Add prosciutto and cook, stirring often, until lightly browned, about 2 minutes. Return asparagus to pot and cook, just to warm through, about 30 seconds.

3   Reduce the heat to low. Stir in the gnocchi, then the mascarpone and Parmesan. Stir just until mascarpone is melted, about 1 minute. Season with salt and freshly ground pepper. Serve, sprinkling a generous shower of basil on each serving.

4 SERVINGS

other ideas

SIMPLE TIP *I have recently seen vacuum-packed diced prosciutto for cooking in my market. If you find it at yours, you can use it instead of getting thickly sliced prosciutto from the deli. You'll need about 1/2 cup diced prosciutto for this recipe.*

VARIATION *Frozen tortellini, either stuffed with cheese or spinach, would be an excellent stand-in for the gnocchi. Frozen gnocchi are only so-so; I prefer the vacuum-packed ones.*

Portobello and Barley Casserole with Dilled Sour Cream

This rib-sticking dish seems made to be served on a cold autumn night. I've resisted the temptation to add meat, as the portobello mushrooms have lots of earthy flavor and don't need any support. I'll be frank—the end result, while very tasty, is an equally earthy brown, but the dilled sour cream adds the necessary contrasting color.

12 ounces portobello mushrooms

1 1/2 cups pearled barley

3 tablespoons butter

1/2 cup finely chopped shallots

3 cups vegetable or chicken broth

2/3 cup sour cream

3 tablespoons chopped fresh dill

PREP *Trim soiled bottoms from mushroom stems. Wipe mushroom caps with a wet paper towel to clean. Cut mushrooms lengthwise, stems and all, into 1/4-inch-thick slices. Place barley in wire sieve and rinse well under cold running water.*

1 Preheat oven to 350°F. Melt butter in 9- or 10-inch ovenproof skillet over medium heat. Add mushrooms and cook, stirring often, until they give off their liquid and it

evaporates, about 10 minutes. Add shallots and cook, stirring often, until they soften, about 1 minute.

2   Add broth and bring to boil, scraping up the browned bits in skillet. Stir in barley, 1 teaspoon salt, and $1/4$ teaspoon freshly ground pepper and return liquid to boil. Cover the skillet.

3   Bake until barley is tender and has absorbed the liquid, about 35 minutes. Mix sour cream and dill in a small bowl. Serve, topping each serving with a dollop of the sour cream.

4 TO 6 SERVINGS

other ideas

SIMPLE TIP *For quicker cooking and better texture, be sure to use pearled barley, where the bran has been polished away from each grain. Hulled barley is somewhat more nutritious but takes much longer to cook. If you use hulled barley, expect an extra hour of cooking and add more broth or water as needed.*

DRESS IT UP *For an even deeper mushroom flavor, stir 1 or 2 tablespoons porcini powder, available at specialty grocers, into the cooked mushrooms.*

VARIATION *Cremini mushrooms are actually small versions of the enormous portobello mushrooms. In fact, they are often labeled as "baby portobellos." Thinly sliced cremini can be used here instead of their big brothers, but they aren't quite as deeply flavored.*

Fettuccine with Long-Simmered Bolognese Sauce

Bolognese sauce is all about meat with a little bit of tomatoes, not the other way around. I have a similar recipe in my Italian cookbook, but this one is quite a bit meatier. This version simmers on the back of the stove for a couple of hours, filling the kitchen with the ultimate Italian cooking aroma—simmering pasta sauce. It freezes well, so consider making a double batch and storing half for a future meal.

2 pounds meat loaf mix (equal amounts of beef, veal, and pork)

1 medium onion, chopped

One 14 1/2-ounce can chopped tomatoes in juice

1/2 cup hearty red wine, such as Zinfandel

3 tablespoons tomato paste

1 1/2 teaspoons Italian seasoning, or 1/2 teaspoon each dried basil, oregano, and rosemary

1 pound fettuccine

Freshly grated Parmesan cheese, for serving

1 Combine meat loaf mix and onion in heavy-bottomed medium saucepan over medium heat. Cook, stirring often, breaking up meat with a spoon, until the meat loses its

raw look, about 10 minutes. Tilt pan to drain off fat. Add tomatoes with juices, wine, tomato paste, and Italian seasoning. Bring to a boil over high heat. Reduce heat to low and simmer, uncovered, until sauce reduces by about one-third, about 2 hours. Season generously with salt and pepper.

2 Meanwhile, bring a large pot of salted water to a boil over high heat. Add the pasta and cook until al dente, about 9 minutes. Drain, then return to pot over low heat.

3 Add 2 cups sauce to pasta and heat 30 to 60 seconds, stirring. Serve pasta topped with more sauce. Pass cheese on the side.

4 TO 6 SERVINGS

other ideas

SIMPLE TIP *An Italian seasoning blend of various dried herbs, such as basil, oregano, rosemary, and thyme, is an easy way to add Mediterranean flair to your cooking. Using this mixture instead of just one herb gives a dish more complex flavor. You'll find the blend in the spice rack at the market, or make your own by mixing equal amounts of the herbs listed above, perhaps with a little sage thrown in for good measure.*

DRESS IT UP *For a rich and traditional fillip to the sauce, stir in $1/2$ cup heavy cream during the last few minutes of simmering.*

VARIATION *Cook 2 finely chopped garlic cloves with the meat loaf mix and onions.*

Rotini with Broccoli, Ham, and Cheddar

Here's another variation on the macaroni and cheese theme, this time the all-American combo of ham, broccoli. And like the Penne with Gruyère and Cremini Mushrooms on page 176, it is equally good served from the pot or baked.

$^{1}/_{2}$ pound smoked ham

1 head broccoli

4 tablespoons ($^{1}/_{2}$ stick) butter

$^{1}/_{3}$ cup all-purpose flour

2 cups milk, heated

3 cups shredded sharp Cheddar cheese, about 12 ounces

1 pound rotini

PREP *Cut ham into bite-size pieces. Cut broccoli florets into bite-size pieces. Peel broccoli stems and cut crosswise into $^{1}/_{4}$-inch-thick rounds.*

1 Melt butter in medium saucepan over medium heat. Add ham and cook until lightly browned, about 2 minutes. Sprinkle with flour and stir well. Gradually stir in milk and bring to a simmer. Reduce heat to low and simmer for 5 minutes. Add Cheddar and stir to melt. Season with salt and pepper to taste. Remove from heat and cover to keep warm.

2 Meanwhile, bring a large pot of lightly salted water to a boil over high heat. Add broccoli stems to water and cook for 2 minutes. Add florets and cook with stems until broccoli is barely tender, about 4 minutes more. Using a skimmer or a wire sieve, scoop broccoli out of water and place in bowl. Add rotini to the same boiling water and cook until al dente, about 9 minutes. Drain rotini, and return rotini and broccoli to pot.

3 Add sauce to pasta and stir well. Cook over low heat until sauce barely simmers. Serve hot.

4 TO 6 SERVINGS

other ideas

DRESS IT UP *Would you like to try this pasta baked? Boil the pasta until it is almost, but not quite, al dente, about 7 minutes (it will cook further in the oven). Drain well. Spread the pasta and sauce in a buttered baking dish. Sprinkle with 3 tablespoons plain dry bread crumbs and dot with 1 tablespoon butter. Bake in a preheated 375°F oven until the top is golden, about 20 minutes.*

VARIATION *Broccoli and cauliflower are close cousins, and the latter would be great in this dish. Cut cauliflower head into bite-size pieces, and cook in the water instead of the broccoli.*

All-American Carbonara with Corn, Bacon, and Jalapeño

Traditional pasta carbonara, named for the coal miners who popularized it, is always made with bacon (or a reasonable Italian version thereof). In my star-spangled version, I've added corn and jalapeño, and they go beautifully with the smoky pork.

1 jalapeño

5 bacon slices

2 cups fresh or thawed frozen corn kernels

$2/3$ cup heavy cream

1 pound fettuccine

3 large eggs

1 cup freshly grated Parmesan cheese, plus more for serving

Chopped fresh cilantro, for serving

PREP *Cut out and discard seeds and ribs from jalapeño; finely chop jalapeño.*

1 Cook bacon in large skillet over medium heat until crisp. Leaving fat in skillet, transfer bacon to paper towels to cool and drain. Return skillet to heat. Add corn and jalapeño and cook, stirring occasionally, until corn begins to brown, about 5 minutes. Stir in cream and bring to a simmer. Remove from heat and keep warm.

2 Meanwhile, bring a large pot of lightly salted water to a boil over high heat. Add fettuccine and cook until barely tender, about 8 minutes. Drain well and return to pot.

3 Coarsely chop bacon. Beat eggs in small bowl. Gradually whisk into warm cream mixture. Pour over fettuccine in pot, then add Parmesan cheese and reserved bacon. Mix well. Season carefully with salt (it could already be salty enough from bacon and cheese) and a generous grinding of pepper. Serve hot, sprinkled with cilantro.

4 TO 6 SERVINGS

other ideas

VARIATION *Add 2 finely chopped garlic cloves to the skillet during the last minute or so of cooking the corn.*

Fettuccine with Chicken, Shiitakes, and Gorgonzola

You can whip this up as an indulgent weeknight meal, or keep it in mind when you need an elegant pasta dish for company. Shiitake mushrooms have just the right meaty flavor to play against the sharp Gorgonzola, but you can use other mushrooms, too. For an extra -special treat, try it with chanterelles.

1 pound boneless and skinless chicken breasts

1 pound shiitake mushrooms

3 tablespoons butter

$^1/_3$ cup chopped shallots

1 cup heavy cream

3 ounces Italian Gorgonzola cheese, preferably "mountain" Gorgonzola

1 pound fettuccine

Freshly grated Parmesan cheese, for serving

PREP *Cut chicken into $^3/_4$-inch pieces. Cut off and discard shiitake stems. Rinse caps, pat dry, and cut into $^1/_2$-inch-wide strips.*

1 Melt 1 tablespoon butter in large skillet over medium heat. Add chicken and cook, stirring occasionally, until chicken is browned and cooked through, about 12 minutes. Season chicken lightly with salt and pepper. Transfer chicken to a plate.

2 Melt remaining 2 tablespoons butter in skillet over medium heat. Add shiitakes and cook, stirring occasionally, until mushrooms begin to give off juices, about 5 minutes. Add shallots and cook until mushrooms are tender, about 5 minutes. Add cream and bring to a boil, scraping up browned bits in skillet. Reduce heat to medium-low and stir in Gorgonzola. Remove from the heat and cover to keep warm.

3 Meanwhile, bring large pot of lightly salted water to boil. Add pasta and cook until al dente, about 8 minutes. Drain and return to pot. Stir in sauce and chicken. Cook over low heat, stirring often, until piping hot, about 1 minute. Season with salt (be careful, the cheese is salty) and a few grinds of black pepper. Serve with the Parmesan passed on the side.

4 TO 6 SERVINGS

other ideas

SIMPLE TIP *Your cheese shop is likely to carry two different versions of Italian Gorgonzola. The "mountain"-style cheese is sharper and easier to crumble, and it makes a stronger statement in cooked dishes. Mild and creamy* dolce de latte *is best reserved for a cheese platter.*

DRESS IT UP *For a splash of herby green color, sprinkle chopped fresh parsley or chives (or a combination of the two) over each serving.*

VARIATION *Turkey breast cutlets, cut into strips, can stand in for the chicken breast. Because turkey breast is so lean, be careful not to overcook it, or it will dry out.*

Spaghetti with Grape Tomatoes and Pesto

Pesto lends its incredibly delicious aroma and flavor to many dishes. Here it is in the role that introduced most of us to its talents—with pasta. Buy pesto from the refrigerated section of the supermarket, as the fresh variety is superior to the bottled version.

1 pound spaghetti
2 tablespoons extra-virgin olive oil
2 pints grape tomatoes
¼ cup store-bought pesto
Freshly grated Parmesan cheese, for serving

1   Bring a large pot of salted water to a boil. Boil spaghetti until al dente, about 9 minutes. Drain, reserving about ½ cup of cooking water. Set pasta aside; do not rinse.

2   Return pot to stove. Add olive oil and heat over medium-high heat. Add tomatoes and cook, stirring occasionally, until tomatoes begin to split, about 3 minutes.

3   Remove pot from heat. Add pasta and pesto. Mix, adding enough reserved cooking water to loosen pesto and create a light sauce. Serve hot, with cheese passed on the side.

4 TO 6 SERVINGS

the simpler the better

SIMPLE TIP *To store leftover pesto, spread it evenly in its container with a spatula. Pour a thin layer of extra-virgin olive oil on top (which seals the pesto and keeps out more air than the lid alone) and refrigerate. When you want to use the pesto, stir in the oil layer. Stored in this manner, the pesto should keep for a couple of weeks.*

DRESS IT UP *Top each serving with crumbled goat cheese.*

VARIATION *Use a few tablespoons of an olive paste, such as tapenade or olivada, instead of the pesto.*

Penne with Gruyère and Cremini Mushrooms

For macaroni and cheese with a European flair, try this warming dish. It doesn't need to be baked, but no one will stop you if you do. Cremini mushrooms, sometimes called baby portobellos, have deeper flavor than white button mushrooms, and they work best with the rich Gruyère cheese.

1 pound penne or another tube-shaped pasta

2 tablespoons butter

10 ounces cremini (baby portobello) mushrooms, thinly sliced

3 tablespoons finely chopped shallots

$^3/_4$ cup heavy cream

3 cups shredded Gruyère cheese, about 12 ounces

$^1/_2$ cup freshly grated Parmesan cheese, plus more for serving

1 Bring a large pot of salted water to a boil over high heat. Add penne and cook until al dente, about 8 minutes. Drain pasta and set aside; do not rinse.

2 Melt butter in medium skillet over medium heat. Add mushrooms and cook, stirring occasionally, until juices evaporate, about 5 minutes. Stir in shallots and cook until tender, about 2 minutes.

3. Return pot to stove. Add cream and bring to a boil over high heat. Reduce heat to medium-low. A handful at a time, stir in Gruyère, letting each batch melt before adding more. Stir in Parmesan. Add pasta and mushrooms and stir well. Season with salt and pepper to taste. Serve hot.

4 TO 6 SERVINGS

other ideas

SIMPLE TIP *A food processor fitted with the coarse shredding blade makes quick work of shredding the Gruyère cheese. For the Parmesan, be sure to use a fine shredding blade, or pulse chunks in the food processor bowl fitted with the metal chopping blade. A good old box grater is a low-tech, but efficient utensil, too.*

DRESS IT UP *Stir a tablespoon or two of porcini powder (pulverized dried porcini mushrooms, available at specialty food stores) into the sautéed mushrooms.*

VARIATION *For a baked version, preheat the oven to 450°F. Cook the penne in the water just until it is almost, but not quite, al dente, about 7 minutes (it will cook further in the oven), and drain the penne well. Spread the mixed penne and sauce into a buttered baking dish. Bake until the ends of the penne are browned, 10 to 15 minutes.*

Italian Kugel with Ricotta, Tomatoes, and Parmesan

In Jewish cooking, every family has its special recipe for noodle kugel. This baked dish is meant to be served as a side dish, but is usually sweet enough to serve as dessert. I've made a luscious savory version, rich with ricotta, eggs, and a topping of plum tomatoes.

4 ripe plum tomatoes

One 12-ounce bag medium-width egg noodles

3 large eggs

One 15- to 16-ounce container ricotta cheese, either whole milk or part skim

1 1/4 cups freshly grated Parmesan cheese

1 tablespoon olive oil

PREP *Cut tomatoes crosswise into 1/3-inch-thick rounds, removing some of the tomato seeds as you slice.*

1 Preheat oven to 350°F. Lightly oil 11 1/2 x 8-inch baking dish. Bring a large pot of lightly salted water to a boil over high heat. Add noodles and cook until barely tender, about 8 minutes. Do not overcook; they will cook more in the oven. Drain noodles well.

2 Whisk eggs in large bowl. Add ricotta, 1 cup Parmesan, $1/2$ teaspoon salt, and $1/4$ teaspoon fresh pepper in a large bowl. Add noodles and mix. Spread in baking dish. Top with rows of sliced tomatoes. Sprinkle with remaining $1/4$ cup Parmesan and drizzle with oil.

3 Bake until kugel feels firm when pressed in center and edges of tomatoes are beginning to brown, about 30 minutes. Let stand 10 minutes before cutting into squares to serve.

6 SERVINGS

other ideas

SIMPLE TIP *Finding ripe tomatoes at the supermarket for the night's meal can be frustrating, as they are more than often underripe. Think ahead and buy tomatoes a few days in advance. Store them uncovered at room temperature. Those hard, pinkish tomatoes may surprise you and ripen into very passable beauties. Because tomatoes have so many uses, tucked into sandwiches, salads, casseroles, and more, it is unlikely that will they get too ripe and go to waste—at least in my kitchen.*

DRESS IT UP *Sprinkle 1 teaspoon chopped fresh thyme over the tomatoes before baking.*

Rigatoni with Lamb Ragù

When many cooks want a pasta sauce, they grab a package of ground beef. Now, that's a good start, but what about ground lamb, which has a much more distinctive and unexpected flavor? Build on the lamb with some of its best companions, like red wine, rosemary, and olives.

1 tablespoon olive oil

1 pound ground lamb

$^1/_2$ cup hearty red wine, such as Zinfandel

One 26-ounce jar marinara sauce

1 tablespoon chopped fresh rosemary, or 1 $^1/_2$ teaspoons dried

$^2/_3$ cup pitted and coarsely chopped Kalamata olives

1 pound rigatoni

$^1/_2$ cup crumbled goat cheese (Chèvre) or feta, about 3 ounces

1   Heat olive oil in large saucepan over medium-high heat. Add lamb and cook, stirring often with wooden spoon to break up meat, until lamb is browned, about 10 minutes. Pour off fat. Add wine and bring to boil. Stir in marinara sauce and rosemary and bring to a simmer. Reduce heat to medium-low and simmer to marry flavors, about 30 minutes. During last 5 minutes of cooking, add olives.

2   Meanwhile, bring a large pot of lightly salted water to a boil over high heat. Add rigatoni and cook until al dente, about 9 minutes. Drain well and return to pot.

3　Add sauce to pasta and mix well. Serve in bowls, topped with crumbled goat cheese.

4 TO 6 SERVINGS

other ideas

SIMPLE TIP *This is one of my few recipes that uses store-bought marinara sauce, as I like to make my own sauce in big batches and freeze it in 1-quart containers. But if it is a good brand, and cooked with full-flavored ingredients that add their own character to the dish, bottled sauce can be a very helpful friend in the kitchen. Look at the label and buy a brand with appetizing ingredients (tomatoes, olive oil, onions, garlic, herbs, and little else) and a self-assured blatant lack of chemicals.*

DRESS IT UP *Pass freshly grated Parmesan cheese at the table, if you wish, but the goat cheese should be enough.*

VARIATION *For a Greek touch, add $1/2$ teaspoon ground cinnamon to the sauce.*

No-Cook Spaghetti Puttanesca

Sassy spaghetti puttanesca, with its in-your-face combination of capers, olives, anchovies, and tuna, quickly established itself as one of the most beloved of all pasta dishes (which is very surprising when you think of the average American palate even twenty years ago). Its speedy preparation could be one of the reasons for its popularity. In this version, the sauce isn't cooked, which is about as fast as you can get.

One 6-ounce can tuna packed in oil, preferably olive oil

4 anchovy fillets

1 pound spaghetti

1 cup ($^1/_2$-inch dice) drained and chopped sun-dried tomatoes in oil, preferably olive oil (reserve 3 tablespoons drained oil)

$^1/_2$ cup pitted and coarsely chopped black Mediterranean olives

3 tablespoons store-bought pesto

2 tablespoons drained nonpareil capers

$^1/_4$ teaspoon crushed red pepper flakes

PREP *Drain tuna, reserving oil. Mince anchovy fillets into a paste.*

1 Bring a large pot of lightly salted water to a boil over high heat. Add spaghetti and cook until al dente, about 9 minutes. Drain, reserving $^1/_2$ cup cooking water.

2 Add sun-dried tomatoes, tuna, olives, pesto, capers, and anchovy fillet paste to pasta cooking pot. Add reserved oil from sun-dried tomatoes and tuna, and stir well, breaking up tuna.

3 Add drained pasta to pot and mix, adding enough reserved cooking water to make a light sauce. Serve hot.

4 TO 6 SERVINGS

other ideas

SIMPLE TIP *Look for sun-dried tomatoes that have been packed in olive oil—they'll have more Italianate flavor than varieties packed in vegetable oil. Or, drain off the vegetable oil and replace the oil in the jar with extra-virgin olive oil. If you can't find sun-dried tomatoes in olive oil, use extra-virgin olive oil when mixing the pasta.*

VARIATION *When plum tomatoes are in season, use them instead of sun-dried tomatoes. Chop 1 pound ripe plum tomatoes into $1/2$-inch dice, shaking out as many seeds as you can as you cut them. Mix the tomatoes in a bowl with the other sauce ingredients and let stand for 30 minutes. Drain the spaghetti, return to the pot, and add the fresh tomato sauce, along with some of the reserved pasta water.*

Rice Noodles with Shrimp and Peanut Sauce

I was only mildly surprised to find an entire array of Thai products in my suburban supermarket, as the way we all cook has changed so much in the last few years. I pounced on a bottle of peanut satay sauce—something that I know how to make from scratch, but which requires quite a few ingredients. The bottled version was delicious and inspired this play on *paad Thai*.

2 tablespoon vegetable oil

1 pound large (21–25 count) shrimp

3 scallions

2 carrots

1 pound wide rice noodles

$1/3$ cup peanut satay sauce

$1 1/3$ cups fresh bean sprouts

Soy sauce, for serving

PREP *Slice green and white parts of scallions. Shred carrots on box grater.*

1 Bring a large pot of lightly salted water to a boil over high heat. Meanwhile, heat oil in large skillet over medium-high heat. Add shrimp and cook until they turn firm and opaque, about 3 minutes. Add scallions and carrots and stir until scallions wilt. Remove from heat and keep warm.

2 When shrimp and vegetables are almost done, add noodles to water. Cook, stirring occasionally to avoid sticking, until noodles are tender, about 6 minutes. Scoop out and reserve $1/2$ cup cooking water. Drain noodles well and rinse under warm water. Return noodles to pot.

3 Add shrimp and vegetables and peanut sauce to noodles. Mix, adding reserved cooking water to thin sauce. Serve hot in bowls, topped with bean sprouts. Pass soy sauce on the side for seasoning.

4 TO 6 SERVINGS

other ideas

SIMPLE TIP *Rice noodles come in a variety of widths. For this recipe, you want rice noodles about $1/2$ inch wide. Thin rice noodles, called rice vermicelli, are too narrow. If the wide rice noodles aren't in the Asian section, look in the pasta aisle, because they are also being marketed as an alternative to flour-based pasta.*

DRESS IT UP *Top each serving with chopped peanuts.*

Risotto with Beef, Tomatoes, and Mozzarella

It's hard to believe that you can get such sophisticated flavor from a humble pound of ground beef. But tasting is believing . . . .

2 garlic cloves

1 large ripe tomato, chopped

2 tablespoons butter

1 pound ground beef round

1 $^1/_2$ cups (11 ounces) rice for risotto, such as arborio

$^1/_2$ cup shredded mozzarella cheese, about 2 ounces

$^1/_2$ cup chopped fresh basil

PREP *Finely chop garlic. Cut tomato into $^1/_2$-inch dice.*

1 Melt butter in medium saucepan over medium heat. Add ground beef and season with $^1/_2$ teaspoon salt and $^1/_4$ teaspoon freshly ground pepper. Cook, stirring occasionally with wooden spoon to break up meat, until beef loses its raw look, about 6 minutes. Add garlic and cook until it gives off its aroma, about 1 minute.

2 Add rice and cook, stirring frequently, until it loses its translucent look, 2 to 3 minutes. Stir in 3 $^3/_4$ cups water and $^1/_2$ teaspoon salt and $^1/_4$ teaspoon freshly ground pepper. Bring to a simmer, stirring occasionally to keep rice from sticking to bottom of pot. Reduce heat to low and cover.

3　Cook until rice is barely al dente, about 11 minutes. Scatter tomato over rice (do not stir) and cover the pot again. Cook until the rice is barely tender and the tomato is heated through, about 3 minutes. Remove from heat. Stir in mozzarella and basil. Serve right away.

4 TO 6 SERVINGS

other ideas

SIMPLE TIP *The starch in medium-grain rice gives risotto its special creaminess. While arborio rice is most commonly available, other varieties, such as carnaroli or vialone nano, are well worth trying the next time you stir a pot of risotto.*

DRESS IT UP *Pass freshly grated Parmesan cheese at the table.*

VARIATION *Use sweet pork or turkey Italian sausage, casings removed, instead of ground round.*

Risotto with Saffron, Shrimp, and Peas

Long ago, I found that you do not have to stir risotto constantly for good results. It is the creamy quality of medium-grain Arborio rice that makes risotto distinctive, so you can make it just like regular steamed rice—as long as the pot has a heavy bottom to prevent scorching. This version fuses the aromatic flavors of paella with the creaminess of risotto.

1 medium onion

$^3/_4$ pound medium (26–30 count) shrimp

2 tablespoons extra-virgin olive oil

1 $^1/_2$ cups (11 ounces) rice for risotto, such as arborio

$^1/_2$ teaspoon crumbled saffron threads

Two 14 $^1/_2$-ounce cans chicken broth

1 cup thawed frozen peas

PREP *Chop onion. Peel and devein shrimp.*

1 Heat olive oil in medium saucepan over medium heat. Add onion and cook, stirring occasionally, until onion softens, about 3 minutes. Add rice and cook, stirring frequently, until it loses its translucent look, 2 to 3 minutes. Stir in saffron.

2   Stir in broth and bring to a simmer, stirring occasionally to keep rice from sticking to bottom of pot. Reduce heat to low and cover.

3   Cook until rice is barely al dente, about 11 minutes. Add shrimp and peas (do not stir) and cover the pot again. Cook until the rice is barely tender and the shrimp is firm and opaque, about 3 minutes. Serve right away with grinds of pepper over the top.

4 TO 6 SERVINGS

other ideas

DRESS IT UP *Ignore the Italian culinary tradition of not serving cheese with fish, and stir 1/2 cup freshly grated Parmesan cheese into the risotto just before serving.*

VARIATION *Before adding the onion, sauté 5 ounces smoked ham, cut into bite-size cubes, in the oil until it is lightly browned, about 3 minutes.*

Stir-Fried Noodles with Pork and Vegetables

It's not always easy to cook Asian dishes with a restricted number of ingredients, as the proper balance of flavors depends on a mixture of small amounts of ingredients. That's why, when pressed for time, I grab a bottle of high-quality stir-fry sauce, which includes ginger, garlic, and other seasonings.

$3/4$ pound boneless pork loin (not tenderloin)

2 medium carrots

2 scallions

9 ounces fresh Chinese noodles

2 tablespoons vegetable oil

2 cups broccoli florets

$1/4$ cup bottled stir-fry sauce

PREP *Cut pork loin crosswise into $1/2$-inch slices; stack and cut again into $1/2$-inch-wide strips. Cut carrots on diagonal into $1/8$-inch-thick slices. Cut scallions (white and green parts) into thin rounds.*

1 Bring a large pot of lightly salted water to a boil over high heat. Add noodles and cook until tender, about 3 minutes. Drain and rinse under cold water; drain well.

2 Heat very large empty skillet over high heat until skillet is very hot, about 2 minutes.

Add 1 tablespoon oil and swirl to coat bottom of skillet. Add pork and cook, stirring often, until browned and cooked through, about 5 minutes. Transfer pork to plate.

3 Heat remaining tablespoon oil in skillet until very hot. Add broccoli and $^1/_4$ cup water. Cover and cook for 1 minute. Add carrots and cook, stirring almost constantly, until carrots are crisp-tender, about 2 minutes. Add reserved pork, noodles, scallions, and stir-fry sauce and mix well. Serve hot in bowls.

4 TO 5 SERVINGS

other ideas

SIMPLE TIP *You'll probably find fresh Chinese noodles in the produce section of the supermarket, next to the egg roll skins. Otherwise, take a look at your local Asian market. You can always use dried spaghetti, cooked until tender, about 9 minutes.*

DRESS IT UP *Add 1 small red bell pepper, seeds and ribs discarded and flesh thinly sliced, to the skillet along with the carrots.*

VARIATION *Try chicken breast, cut into thin strips, instead of the pork.*

the simpler the better Roasted and Grilled Suppers

Roast Beef and Vegetable Dinner

Meat-and-potatoes lovers will love this classic roast with a sharp, creamy sauce to perk things up. Potatoes and carrots are old friends of roast beef, but try other root vegetables such as celery root and parsnips, too.

3 large russet or Burbank baking potatoes

1 pound medium-width carrots

1 scallion

8 thyme sprigs, or $1/2$ teaspoon dried

2 tablespoons vegetable oil

1 beef eye of round, about $2^1/2$ pounds

1 cup sour cream

2 tablespoons prepared horseradish

PREP *Peel potatoes and cut each lengthwise into 8 wedges. Cut carrots into 1-inch lengths. Slice scallion (white and green parts) into thin rounds.*

1 Preheat oven to 400°F. Lightly oil large roasting pan. Combine potatoes, carrots, and thyme in pan and toss with oil. Season with $1/2$ teaspoon salt and $1/4$ teaspoon freshly ground pepper. Make a trough in center of vegetables, and place the beef in trough. Season roast all over with $1/2$ teaspoon salt and $1/2$ teaspoon freshly ground pepper.

2 Roast for 30 minutes. Turn the meat. Scrape up and turn vegetables with metal spatula. Continue roasting until meat thermometer inserted in center of beef reads 125–130°F for medium-rare meat, approximately 30 to 40 minutes more. Transfer meat to a carving board and let stand for 10 minutes. Keep vegetables warm in turned-off oven.

3 Meanwhile, mix sour cream, horseradish, and scallion in small bowl and let stand at room temperature to lose its chill. Carve roast and serve with vegetables and sauce.

6 SERVINGS

other ideas

SIMPLE TIP *Eye of round is very lean and will dry out if roasted much beyond the medium-rare stage, so take care. A reliable meat thermometer is a must in any kitchen. Instant-read thermometers are a good choice. The new digital probe thermometers, while pricey, also give fast readouts. Be sure to place the tip of either thermometer in the true center of the roast. If the tip isn't deep enough, you will get an inaccurate reading.*

VARIATIONS *Substitute parsnips for the carrots.*

Substitute celery root (celeriac) for the potatoes. The celery root should be pared with a small sharp knife before cutting into pieces.

Chili-Rubbed Flank Steak Tacos

Rubbed with a simple blend of chili powder and cumin seeds, the flank steak is excellent on its own. But to stretch it into a main course, slice it and serve with the fixings for soft tacos.

2 teaspoons chili powder

1 teaspoon cumin seeds, crushed in a mortar or under a heavy saucepan

1 flank steak, 1 $^3/_4$ pounds

12 corn tortillas, warmed

2 cups thinly shredded iceberg lettuce

2 cups store-bought salsa

2 large ripe avocados, pitted, peeled, and sliced

$^1/_2$ cup grated Romano cheese

1 Mix $^1/_2$ teaspoon salt, chili powder, and cumin in small bowl. Rub all over flank steak.

2 Build a hot fire in a barbecue grill (or preheat gas grill on High). Lightly oil grill grate. Grill steak over coals, turning once, until browned on both sides, about 8 minutes. Transfer to carving board and let stand 5 minutes.

3 Holding knife at a slant, carve steak crosswise against grain into thin slices. Serve with tortillas, lettuce, salsa, avocados, and Romano cheese, letting each guest make his or her own taco.

4 TO 6 SERVINGS

SIMPLE TIP *All steaks and roasts will benefit from a short rest before carving. As the meat cooks, the heat pushes the juices into the center of the meat. If carved too soon, the collected juices stay in the center, making the end slices less juicy than they could be. Resting allows the juices to redistribute through the meat, with more uniformly moist slices.*

Grilled Lemony Chicken with Asparagus

With a bit of forethought, you can get an entire meal off of the grill. One trick is to heap the coals into a bank, giving hot and cooler areas for cooking. After browning the chicken over the hot coals, the chicken is moved to the cooler area to finish, freeing up the hot area to grill the asparagus. The lemon marinade is a keeper.

2 garlic cloves

4 boneless and skinless chicken breasts, about 7 ounces each

1 pound asparagus

$1/2$ cup freshly squeezed lemon juice

$1/3$ cup plus 2 tablespoons extra-virgin olive oil

1 tablespoon Dijon mustard

1 teaspoon herbes de Provence (see *Simple Tip,* page 59), or $1/4$ teaspoon each dried thyme, basil, rosemary, and sage

PREP *Crush garlic under a knife and peel. Lightly pound chicken breasts to even thickness with meat pounder or heel of your hand. Snap off woody ends of asparagus.*

1 Mix lemon juice, $1/3$ cup olive oil, mustard, herbes de Provence, garlic, $1/4$ teaspoon salt, and $1/4$ teaspoon freshly ground pepper in 1-quart zipper-seal plastic bag. Add chicken, close bag, and refrigerate while preparing barbecue grill, but no longer than 30 minutes or so. In another plastic bag, toss asparagus with remaining 2 tablespoons olive oil.

2 Build a hot fire in a barbecue grill (or preheat gas grill on high). Spread coals in a bank, with a double thickness of coals on one side of grill and a single thickness on the other. (On a gas grill, keep one burner on high and the other on low.) Lightly oil grill grate. Grill chicken over the hot, thick bank of coals (high burner), until the underside is seared with brown grid marks, about 2 minutes. Turn and repeat on the other side, about 2 minutes more. Move chicken to the cooler, thin bank of coals (low burner). Grill until chicken feels firm when pressed in the center, about 10 minutes.

3 After chicken has grilled for 5 minutes, arrange asparagus over hot coals (high burner), with spears perpendicular to grid so they don't fall through. Grill, rolling asparagus occasionally on grid to turn and cook evenly on all sides, until crisp-tender, about 5 minutes depending on thickness of asparagus. Use a metal spatula to transfer asparagus to platter. Season asparagus with salt and freshly ground pepper to taste. Transfer chicken to platter and serve.

4 SERVINGS

other ideas

SIMPLE TIP *Marinating is a good flavor booster, but too much of a good thing can be bad. A marinade will only penetrate $1/8$ inch or less into food, no matter how long you let the food soak. When protein foods like meat, poultry, or seafood come into contact with the acidic ingredient in a marinade (be it lemon juice, wine, or vinegar), the protein softens, giving the food a mushy texture. Most foods need only a short soak—a half hour usually is plenty.*

Roast Chicken with Mediterranean Vegetables

Here, many Mediterranean flavors combine to make a an unusual contribution to the roast chicken canon.

1 medium eggplant, about 1 1/2 pounds

3 medium zucchini, well scrubbed

6 ripe plum tomatoes

6 garlic cloves

3 tablespoons extra-virgin olive oil

1 large chicken, about 4 1/2 pounds, quartered

1 teaspoon herbes de Provence (see *Simple Tip*, page 59), or 1/2 teaspoon each dried basil and dried rosemary

PREP *Cut eggplant into 1-inch chunks. Cut each zucchini lengthwise in half, and then crosswise into 1-inch-wide pieces. Cut each tomato in half lengthwise. Crush garlic under a large knife and peel.*

1 Preheat oven to 400°F. Lightly oil a large flameproof roasting pan. Combine eggplant, zucchini, tomatoes, and garlic in pan and toss with 2 tablespoons olive oil. Season with 1/2 teaspoon salt and 1/4 teaspoon freshly ground pepper. Season chicken quarters with 1/2 teaspoon salt and 1/2 teaspoon freshly ground pepper. Place on vegetables, drizzle with remaining tablespoon olive oil, and sprinkle herbs de Provence over all.

2 Roast, occasionally stirring the vegetables under chicken, until chicken shows no sign of pink when pierced at the drumstick bone with tip of knife, about 1 hour. Transfer chicken to serving platter and tent with aluminum foil to keep warm.

3 Place roasting pan with vegetables over 2 burners on medium-high heat. Cook, stirring occasionally, until vegetables juices thicken, 3 to 5 minutes. Serve chicken with vegetables.

4 SERVINGS

other ideas

SIMPLE TIP *When eggplant isn't quite fresh, it can be a little bitter. Luckily, there is an easy trick for mellowing its sharpness. If you have doubts about your eggplant's flavor, sprinkle the eggplant with 1 teaspoon salt (preferably kosher salt) in a colander, and let the eggplant stand for 1 hour to drain off any bitter juices. Rinse the eggplant well under cold running water and pat dry with paper towels. Now proceed with the recipe as directed.*

VARIATION *Add $1/2$ cup pitted Kalamata olives to the vegetables when you finish them on the stove.*

Curry-Crusted Leg of Lamb with Roasted Cauliflower and Carrots

Most people are surprised to find that yogurt is a wonderful way to add flavor to meats. Mixed with curry powder and garlic and slathered on boneless leg of lamb, it melts away during roasting to leave behind a savory crust on the meat. Cauliflower and carrots cook alongside to complete the picture.

1 head cauliflower

2 garlic cloves

1 pound baby-cut carrots

2 tablespoons vegetable oil

1 boneless leg of lamb, trimmed, about $2\frac{1}{2}$ pounds

$\frac{1}{2}$ cup plain low-fat yogurt

2 teaspoons Madras-style curry powder

3 tablespoons chopped fresh mint

PREP *Break cauliflower into florets. Crush garlic through a press.*

1 Preheat oven to 400°F. Lightly oil large roasting pan. Place carrots and cauliflower in pan. Toss with oil, $\frac{1}{2}$ teaspoon salt, and $\frac{1}{4}$ teaspoon freshly ground pepper. Season lamb with $\frac{1}{2}$ teaspoon salt. Make a trough in vegetables and place lamb in trough. Mix yogurt, curry powder, and garlic in small bowl. Spread evenly over lamb.

2 Roast, occasionally stirring vegetables, until vegetables are barely tender and meat thermometer inserted in thickest part of lamb reads 130°F for medium-rare lamb, about 35 minutes. Transfer lamb to carving board and let stand 10 minutes. Keep vegetables warm in turned-off oven.

3 Carve lamb crosswise into thin slices. Transfer lamb and juices to one side of serving platter. Heap vegetables on other side of platter. Sprinkle mint over all. Serve hot.

6 SERVINGS

other ideas

SIMPLE TIP *Madras-style curry powder is mildly spicy, with turmeric as one of its main ingredients. It's the one that you'll find most easily in supermarkets. There are many different types of curry powder with a huge variety of spice blends, and if you live in a large city with a spice store, you can experiment with them.*

Pesto Monkfish with Potatoes and Zucchini

Pesto comes to the rescue here to give meaty monkfish a zesty crust. This recipe is one of the reasons I always have a container of pesto in my refrigerator.

1 $^1/_2$ pounds red-skinned or Yukon Gold potatoes, scrubbed

2 medium zucchini

3 tablespoons extra-virgin olive oil

4 monkfish fillets, about 7 ounces each

4 tablespoons store-bought pesto

$^1/_2$ cup freshly grated Parmesan cheese

PREP *Cut potatoes into 1-inch pieces. Cut zucchini lengthwise in half, then crosswise into $^1/_4$-inch-thick pieces.*

1 Preheat oven to 400°F. Lightly oil large baking sheet. In pan, toss potatoes with 2 tablespoons olive oil, $^1/_2$ teaspoon salt, and $^1/_4$ teaspoon freshly ground pepper. Roast for 30 minutes.

2 Remove pan from oven. Toss zucchini with remaining tablespoon olive oil, and mix with potatoes. Season monkfish with $^1/_4$ teaspoon salt and $^1/_4$ teaspoon freshly ground pepper. Place on top of potatoes and zucchini. Spread each fillet with 1 tablespoon pesto. Return to oven and roast until vegetables are tender and monkfish

looks opaque in center when pierced with tip of knife, 25 to 30 minutes. Transfer fish to one side of serving platter and tent with foil to keep warm.

3   Sprinkle Parmesan over vegetables in pan. Roast just until cheese melts, about 3 minutes. Heap vegetables on other side of platter and serve.

4 SERVINGS

Roast Jerk Pork with Yams and Watercress

Jerk, the essential Jamaican seasoning, is created from quite a collection of ingredients—scallions, allspice, and really hot Scotch bonnet chiles are the main flavors—but it all comes together into a miraculous paste. Here, it is rubbed onto pork loin, then roasted with orange-fleshed yams. Be sure to choose long narrow yams, which will cook more quickly than thick, stubby ones. During the last few minutes, watercress is tossed into the pan to wilt, making another surprisingly good combination of tastes.

2 1/2 pounds orange-fleshed yams (sweet potatoes), such as Jewel or Garnet

2 tablespoons vegetable oil

1 tablespoon jerk seasoning

1 boneless pork loin roast (not tenderloin), about 2 pounds, tied

3 bunches (6 ounces each) watercress, tough stems discarded, well rinsed

PREP *Peel yams and cut into 3/4-inch-thick rounds.*

1 Preheat oven to 400°F. Lightly oil large roasting pan. Place yams in pan, drizzle with 1 tablespoon oil, and season with 1/2 teaspoon salt and 1/4 teaspoon freshly ground pepper. Toss well. Mix jerk seasoning and remaining tablespoon oil. Spread all over the pork roast.

2 Make a trough in center of yams and place pork in trough. Roast for 30 minutes. Turn roast and stir yams. Continue roasting until meat thermometer inserted in center of roast reads 150°F, 20 to 30 minutes more. Transfer pork to carving board and tent with aluminum foil to keep warm.

3 Push yams to one side of the pan. Mound watercress in empty area of pan and season with $1/2$ teaspoon salt. Return to oven and roast, stirring watercress every few minutes, until it wilts, about 10 minutes. Carve pork and serve with yams and watercress.

4 TO 6 SERVINGS

other ideas

SIMPLE TIP *Jerk seasoning varies greatly from brand to brand, especially in saltiness. If you are trying an unfamiliar brand, spread a bit on a cracker or a piece of cooked meat to assess its salt content and heat level. Jerk seasoning is a wet paste, not a dry rub, so pass over dry spice mixtures that are labeled "jerk."*

Spice-Rubbed Ribs with Roasted Corn

A few well-chosen ingredients, an oven, a pan, and . . . dinner! It should always be this simple, and this delicious.

4 ears of corn

4 pounds pork spareribs, cut into slabs as needed to fit pan

4 teaspoons salt-free Cajun seasoning

PREP *Husk corn and remove silk. Break or cut each ear in half crosswise.*

1 Preheat oven to 350°F. Lightly oil large roasting pan. Season ribs all over with the Cajun seasoning and 2 teaspoons salt. Arrange ribs, overlapping as needed, in pan.

2 Roast for 1 hour. Turn ribs and roast for 30 minutes more.

3 Remove pan from oven. Place corn around ribs, rolling ears to coat in juices. Roast until ribs and corn are tender, about 30 minutes more. Transfer ribs to carving board and let stand 5 minutes. Cut into individual ribs and serve with corn.

4 SERVINGS

SIMPLE TIP *Cajun seasoning should be a mix of herbs and spices without any salt. Watch out for Creole seasoning, which is usually mostly salt with a bit of other seasonings. If you want to make your own Cajun seasoning, mix 2 tablespoons sweet paprika, 1 tablespoon each dried basil and thyme, 1 teaspoon each garlic powder and onion powder, $1/2$ teaspoon freshly ground pepper, and $1/4$ teaspoon ground red (cayenne) pepper.*

DRESS IT UP *Spread your favorite barbecue sauce on the rib, if you like. During the 30 minutes of roasting, brush or slather the sauce on the ribs. Roast the ribs for 15 minutes, then turn the slab and brush the sauce on the other side. Roast for 15 minutes more.*

VARIATION *Substitute baby back ribs for the spareribs, adjusting the cooking time. Roast the baby back ribs for 1 hour, then add the corn to make a total cooking time of $1 1/2$ hours.*

Slow-Roasted Pork Sandwiches with Sweet Slaw

Save this leisurely cooked meal for a weekend afternoon when you might have a little extra time on your hands. Slow-cooking melts the tough parts of the pork shoulder, basting it from the inside out, and the result is fork-tender pork. Heaped on a bun and topped with slaw, it's so tasty that you won't need sauce.

$^1/_2$ cup plus 1 tablespoon vegetable oil

$^1/_2$ pork shoulder roast with skin and bone, about 4 $^1/_2$ pounds
    (see *Simple Tip*, page 211)

2 tablespoons cider vinegar

1 tablespoon sugar

One 16-ounce bag cole slaw mix

2 teaspoons hickory-smoke flavoring (optional)

8 sandwich rolls

1   Preheat oven to 300°F. Heat 1 tablespoon oil in Dutch oven over medium-high heat. Season pork with 1 teaspoon salt and $^1/_2$ teaspoon freshly ground pepper. Add pork to Dutch oven and cook, turning occasionally, until browned on all sides, about 10 minutes. Cover tightly. Bake, allowing roast to create its own juices, until meat is very tender, 2 $^1/_2$ to 3 hours.

2 Meanwhile, whisk vinegar, sugar, $1/2$ teaspoon salt, and $1/4$ teaspoon freshly ground pepper in medium bowl. Gradually whisk in remaining $1/2$ cup oil. Add cole slaw mix and mix well. Cover and refrigerate until ready to use.

3 Transfer pork to carving board. Let stand 20 minutes. Cut off and remove skin and excess fat. Using 2 forks, pull pork into shreds. Transfer to bowl. If desired, season pork with smoke flavoring. Heap pork onto buns, top with slaw, and serve.

8 SERVINGS

other ideas

SIMPLE TIP *Pork shoulder, sometimes called* pernil *or* cala *in Latino markets, is a very large cut—it can run up to 10 pounds. That's fine for serving a crowd but too big for average family meals, even though this roast will shrink considerably during cooking. Many supermarkets carry half-shoulders, which are much more manageable. If your butcher has only the full-size shoulder, ask to have it cut in half and freeze the other portion for another meal.*

Tuscan Roast Pork with Root Vegetables

At outdoor markets all over Tuscany, you'll always find a stand selling roast or grilled pork seasoned with lots of garlic and rosemary. I like to roast it with sweet root vegetables to make a one-dish meal.

1 pound red-skinned or Yukon Gold potatoes, scrubbed

1 pound turnips

1 pound parsnips

2 garlic cloves, crushed through a press

1 tablespoon chopped fresh rosemary

1 boneless pork loin roast, about 2 $^1/_2$ pounds, tied

3 tablespoons extra-virgin olive oil

$^3/_4$ cup chicken broth

PREP *Cut potatoes into 1-inch chunks. Peel turnips and parsnips and cut into 1-inch chunks.*

1 Preheat oven to 350°F. Lightly oil large roasting pan. Mix garlic, rosemary, $^1/_4$ teaspoon salt, and a few grinds of pepper in small bowl. Make 8 slits about 1 inch deep with tip of knife all over pork roast. Force garlic-rosemary mixture into slits. Rub pork with 1 tablespoon olive oil and season with $^1/_2$ teaspoon salt and $^1/_4$ teaspoon freshly ground pepper.

2 Place potatoes, turnips, and parsnips in pan. Toss with remaining 2 tablespoons olive

oil, $1/2$ teaspoon salt, and $1/4$ teaspoon freshly ground pepper. Make a trough in center of vegetables, and place roast in trough. Bake, occasionally stirring vegetables, for 1 hour. Increase oven temperature to 400°F and roast until vegetables are browned and tender and meat thermometer inserted in center of roast reads 145°F, about 20 minutes more. Transfer roast to carving board and let stand 10 minutes. Keep vegetables warm in turned-off oven.

3 Carve roast and transfer to one side of serving platter. Heap vegetables on other side of platter. Tent with foil to keep warm. Place roasting pan over 2 burners on high heat. Add broth and bring to a boil, scraping up browned bits in pan with wooden spatula. Cook until broth is evaporated by half, about 3 minutes. Pour over pork and serve.

6 SERVINGS

other ideas

SIMPLE TIP *There are times when dried herbs are perfectly fine. For example, dried oregano in tomato sauce is classic and tastes different from fresh oregano, which isn't as sharp. But this recipe isn't one of those times. I don't know any cooks who went back to dried herbs after they learned to cook with fresh.*

Roast Salmon with Mustard Crumbs, Fennel, and Red Peppers

You can talk about poached or grilled salmon all you wish—nothing brings out the natural flavor of salmon like roasting. The mustard crumbs are almost ridiculously simple to apply.

3 fennel bulbs, about 2 pounds total

2 roasted red bell peppers

3 tablespoons extra-virgin olive oil

2 pounds center-cut salmon fillet

3 tablespoons grainy mustard, such as moutarde de Meux

$^3/_4$ cup fresh bread crumbs

Lemon wedges, for serving

PREP *Trim fronds from fennel. Coarsely chop and reserve. Cut each fennel bulb in half. Cut out and discard hard triangular core. Cut fennel crosswise into $^1/_4$-inch-thick slices. Coarsely chop red peppers.*

1 Preheat oven to 400°F. Lightly oil large roasting pan. Toss fennel in pan with 2 tablespoons olive oil, $^1/_2$ teaspoon salt, and $^1/_4$ teaspoon freshly ground pepper. Roast for 10 minutes.

2 Remove pan from oven. Stir red pepper into fennel. Place salmon on vegetables.

Spread with mustard and sprinkle evenly with bread crumbs, pressing to make them adhere to salmon. Drizzle with remaining tablespoon olive oil.

3   Return pan to oven and bake until crumbs are browned, fennel is crisp-tender, and salmon is barely opaque when pierced in center with tip of knife, about 25 minutes. Serve from pan, with the lemon wedges.

4 SERVINGS

other ideas

SIMPLE TIP *To make bread crumbs, start with firm white bread—if it is a day or two old, so much the better. There's no need to remove the crusts. Just break up the bread and process it in a food processor or blender until you get coarse crumbs. An average-size slice of white bread yields about $1/3$ cup crumbs.*

Index